A JOURNEY OF A THOUSAND MILES

TASNEEM KARA

A JOURNEY OF A THOUSAND MILES

"From Allah, Through Allah, To Allah"

A Story of a Little
Girl's Quest for Love

A JOURNEY OF A THOUSAND MILES
From Allah, Through Allah, To Allah
A Story of a Little Girl's Quest for Love

First Edition, First Imprint 2025
ISBN: 978-1-0370-9896-3
Copyright © Tasneem Kara

Editor: Sigwa Mafu

Published by: Inspired Publishing
PO Box 82058 | Southdale | 2135 Johannesburg, South Africa Email: info@inspiredpublishing.co.za | www.inspiredpublishing.co.za

© All rights are reserved. Apart from any fair dealing for the purpose of research, criticism or review as permitted under the Copyright Act, no part of this publication may be reproduced, stored in a retrieval system or transmitted, in any form or by any means, electronic, mechanical, photocopying, recording, or otherwise, without the prior written permission of the copyright holder.

GLOSSARY

Islamic Phrases

1. **As-salamu alaykum:** "Peace be upon you."
2. **Bismillah ir-Rahman ir-Rahim:** "In the name of Allah, the Most Gracious, the Most Merciful."
3. **Subhanallah:** "Glory be to Allah"
4. **Alhamdulillah:** "All praise be to Allah"
5. **Allahu Akbar:** "Allah is the Greatest"
6. **La ilaha illallah Muhammadur Rasulullah:** "There is no god but Allah, and Muhammad is the Messenger of Allah."

Honorifics

1. **SWT (Subhanahu Wa Ta'ala):** "The Most Glorified and Exalted"
2. **PBUH (Peace Be Upon Him):** Used after mentioning the Prophet Muhammad's name.
3. **AS (Alayhis Salaam):** "Peace be upon him"
4. **SAW (Sallallahu Alayhi Wa Sallam):** "May Allah's peace and blessings be upon him"
5. **RA (Radi Allahu Anha):** "May Allah be pleased with her"

Islamic Concepts

1. **Allah/Rabb:** "God" or "Lord"

2. **Deen:** Way of life, faith, or religion
3. **Fitrah:** Innate nature or natural disposition
4. **Jannah:** "Paradise" or "Heaven"
5. **Jahannam:** "Hell" or "Hellfire"
6. **Dunya:** "This world"
7. **Akhirah:** "The Hereafter" or "the afterlife"

Other Terms

1. **Shukran:** "Thank you"
2. **Ayah:** "Signs" or "verses"
3. **Shaytan:** "Satan" or "the Devil"
4. **Dua:** "Supplication" or "prayer"
5. **Salah:** "Prayer" or "worship"
6. **Hajj:** A pilgrimage to Mecca
7. **Umrah:** A voluntary pilgrimage to Mecca
8. **Ramadan:** A month of fasting
9. **Eid al-Fitr:** A joyous Islamic holiday marking the end of Ramadan
10. **Eid al-Adha:** A festival of sacrifice
11. **Nafs:** "Self" or "soul"
12. **Halaal:** "Permissible" or "lawful"
13. **Haram:** "Forbidden" or "unlawful"

Quran and Hadith

1. **Quran:** The holy book of Islam
2. **Hadith:** Sayings and actions of the Prophet Muhammad

3. **Tirmidhi, Sahih Muslim, Sahih Bukhari:** Collections of Hadith

Names of Allah

1. **Al Jabbar:** The Compeller
2. **Al Qadir:** The Powerful
3. **Al Latif:** The Gentle
4. **Al Wahid:** The One - emphasising Allah's unity and uniqueness

Family Terms

1. **Dada:** "Grandfather"
2. **Dadi:** "Grandmother"

Other

1. **Surah:** A chapter in the Quran

"Bismillah ir-Rahman ir-Rahim"

Dedication

Ya Rabb, Alhumdulilah for EVERYTHING!

I humbly dedicate this book of poetry to You, my Beloved Rabb. Your divine guidance and wisdom have inspired every word, every thought, and every emotion that has been poured into these pages. I am forever grateful for the unwavering love and support You have shown me, giving me the strength and courage to put pen to paper and complete this, my very first book.

May these words be a source of inspiration, comfort, and guidance for all who read them, reminding us that we are all connected as Your creation. May my words be a reflection of Your beauty, mercy, and wisdom. May they bring joy, peace, and tranquillity to the hearts of those who read them. I ask that You accept this humble effort and make it a means of spreading love, kindness, and compassion throughout this Dunya.

As I reflect on my life's journey, I am reminded that every experience, every person who has touched my life, has been decreed by You for my greater good. Subhanallah.

"And indeed, with hardship comes ease." (Quran 94:5)

This ayat is a gentle reminder that every challenge is a seed of growth; every struggle is a chance to unfurl our wings; and every hardship is an opportunity to discover the beauty of transformation. May we all find solace in these words, like a soft blanket that wraps our souls in comfort and peace.

I extend my heartfelt gratitude to our beloved Prophet Muhammad (peace be upon him), whose teachings have transformed my life, guiding me towards compassion, kindness, and wisdom.

His example has been a beacon of light, inspiring me to become a better version of myself. I am forever grateful for the gift of his teachings.

To my loving husband, my partner, my best friend, and my soulmate, shukran for being my forever home. You are the sunshine that brightens every day, the calm in every storm, and the safe haven where I can always find peace. I am forever grateful that we get to walk this journey together, now and forever, until we meet at Jannah's gate.

Ameen.

Acknowledgements

To my beloved mothers, who taught me the meaning of strength, sacrifice, and unconditional love, shukran, for being my shelter, and my guiding star. Your influence has shaped me into the woman I am today, and I am forever grateful for the lessons you've taught me. We love you both, and you are dearly missed. Until we meet at Jannah's gate.

To our handsome hero son and beautiful independent daughters, who have brought so much joy and light into our lives, shukran, for being our greatest blessings. You are the reason we keep going, the reason we keep striving to be better, and the reason we are so proud to be your parents. May we continue to strengthen our bonds and love for each other.

To our lovely daughter-in-law, who has become an integral part of our family, shukran for birthing two beautiful granddaughters, bringing goodness and adding value to our lives. You are appreciated more than words can ever express.

To our rare gems, our granddaughters, who are the apples of our eye, shukran for being the sparkle in our eyes. You are the wetness in our mouths, the smile on our faces, and the love in our hearts. We are so grateful to be your Dada and Dadi.

To our dear sisters, who have been our confidantes, our partners in crime, and our lifelong friends, shukran to you both for being a constant source of love, support, and encouragement in our lives. Your presence in our lives has been a blessing, and we cherish the memories we've shared together. May there be many more years that we get to walk together.

To my late brother-in-law, who has filled the role of a father, mentor and guide, no amount of words will ever be enough to show my gratitude for what you have done for me. May Allah Subhanahu Wa Ta'ala, reward you tenfold for the role you played in my life. You are dearly missed, until we meet at Jannah's gate.

To my beloved extended family, I am glad that we get to walk, explore, and experience this life's journey with you all. Every step, every moment, and every memory we've shared has been a treasure to me. I cherish our laughter, our tears, and our moments of silence. I cherish our love, our support, and our unwavering commitment to one another.

To every person who has walked alongside me, sharing in my joys and sorrows, shukran, for being a part of my life's journey. Whether your presence was for growth or for support, I am grateful for the impact you've had on my life.

To those who have challenged me, pushed me to grow, and forced me to confront my weaknesses, shukran for helping me discover my strength, my resilience, and my capacity to love. Your presence in my life has been a blessing, even if it didn't always feel that way at the time.

May Allah (SWT), bless you dear readers, with love, laughter and happiness. May he guide you, comfort you, and inspire you to draw closer to Him. May my story be a reminder that you are never alone, and that Allah (SWT) is always with you, guiding you, and loving you. Ameen.

A Message of Hope

Through my book, I invite you to embark on a journey of self-discovery, personal growth, healing, evolving, and thriving. My poetry and story are a testament to the human spirit's capacity for resilience, hope, love, and transformation. May my words inspire you to deepen your faith, cultivate meaningful relationships, and live a life that reflects your values and purpose. May you learn to trust in our one true Rabb "Al Wahid" and may your spirit be lifted by the knowledge that you are loved and cherished.

Introduction

Asalam-walykum and Welcome to a journey of the heart, a journey that weaves together the threads of love, faith, and resilience. In the midst of life's storms, I found solace in the beauty of words and the warmth of faith. This collection of poems is a testament to the power of the human spirit to transform pain into purpose and to find meaning and fulfilment in the most unexpected places. As you read these words, I invite you to reflect on your own journey, to explore the depths of your soul, and to discover the beauty that lies within.

May these poems be a source of comfort, strength, and inspiration for you, and may they guide you on your own path towards purpose, passion, and fulfilment. Let us embark on this journey together, with hearts full of hope and spirits full of love, and may our Rabb guide us every step of the way. Ameen.

Contents

Glossary 5
Dedication 9
Acknowledgements 11
A Message of Hope 14

Introduction 15
"A Journey of a Thousand Miles" 20
"A Little Girl's Quest for Love" 21

Part 1
Poems of Faith and Spirituality 25
"Echoes of The Soul" 30
"Reach Out, For Allah (Swt) Is Near" 33
"Ya Rabb, My Beloved Rabb" 37
"The Call to Prayer" 41
"Find Your Calm Spirit" 45
"You Do You and I'll Do Me" 48
"Beware of Shaytan's Whispers" 52
"I See You, Oh Allah (Swt)" 56

Part 2
Poems of Love And Connection 63
"Threads Of Love" 68
"Our Dearest Treasures, Our Loving Mums" 72
"A Sister's Love" 76
"Oh Sister, Oh Sister" 80
"Friends: Rare Gems From Above" 84
"A Guardian Angel, Sent From Above" 87
"Brothers Of Blood" 91
"A Message To My Father" 96
"Home Is Where The Heart Is, The Best Of You" 101
"A Mother's Love" 105

Part 3
Poems Of Hope And Resilience 111
"A Mixed Heritage, A Unique Soul" 116
"When Delays Are Blessings" 120
"When Darkness Fades, Allah's Light Prevails" 124
"A Journey Of Healing" 128
"Journeying Through Life Guided By Faith" 131
"Women Of Islam" 135
"Living With Purpose" 139
"Taking Back Control (Nafs/Ego)" 142
"Dedication To All Believers" 145
"Society's Expectations Vs. Allah's Pleasure" 148

Part 4
Poems Of Reflection And Growth (Journey Within) 153
"Chasing Sunsets To The Ends Of The Earth" 158
"Tribute To The Chosen Ones" 161
"Establishing Healthy Boundaries" 165
"You Can't Fix Yourself By Hurting Others" 168
"Life's Journey Of Growth" 171
"Our Children Are Blessings, Not Possessions" 174
"Be Good To Your Parents" 178
"Valuing The Efforts Of Others" 182

Part 5
Poems Of Self-Discovery And Healing 187
"My Mind And Me" 192
"A Love Letter To Myself: Be Kind To Yourself" 195
"Healing Rain" 199
"As You Evolve" 202
"Forgiveness: The Best Form Of Love" 205
"Embracing My Broken Pieces" 208
"Moving On" 211
"Embracing My True Self" 214
"Reflection On Self-Care And Self-Love" 218
"Al Quran, A Gift Divine" 221

Part 6
Poems Of Social Awareness And Justice 227

"A Prayer For The People Of Gaza" 232

"When Genocide Becomes A Memory" 236

"Don't Be Swayed: Halaal/Haram" 239

"Words Are Energy, Choose Yours Wisely" 242

"Respect: A Priceless Gift" 245

"Show Up Authentically" 248

"Treat Others With Kindness" 251

"Gift Of Giving, A Blessing Divine" 254

"Smile, It's A Sunnah" 257

"Living In The Dark" 260

Part 7
Poems Of Remembrance And Gratitude 265

"A Heart's Awakening" 270

"Alhumdulillah, For My Life Partner, Best Friend And Love" 274

"My Divine Purpose" 278

"Alhumdulillah" 281

"Our Beloved Prophet Muhammad (Pbuh)" 284

"Gratitude" 288

"The Beauty Of Islam" 291

Parting Words 300

"A Journey of a Thousand Miles"

From Allah, Through Allah, To Allah:
A Little Girl's Quest For Love

Asalam-walykum and welcome to my sacred space, where words meet heart and soul.

In the whispers of the wind, where shadows dance and memories linger, a little girl's quest for love and belonging unfolds. Like a delicate petal, her heart beats with a deep longing, searching for the warmth of acceptance and the gentle touch of connection. This is the essence of **"A Little Girl's Quest for Love,"** a powerful and emotional exploration of the universal human experience.

As I share my story of transformation and healing through Allah's love, I invite you to reflect on your own journey. May these words bring you solace, comfort, and peace, illuminating your path with guidance and wisdom. May Allah's love and mercy surround you, touching your heart and inspiring your soul. Ameen.

"A Little Girl's Quest for Love"

In tiny hands, a heart once beat with a deep desire
A five-year-old's quest for love, a journey to acquire
She wandered, lost, through life's busy streets
Seeking warmth, a gentle touch, a love that meets

Years went by, like falling leaves, her search continued
Through joy and grief, she chased the wind, only to find
A hollow echo, an empty mind, until one day
A family bloomed, a love so bright, lit up her way

A husband's arms, a haven to rest, children's laughter, a heart now blessed
Yet, amidst this joy, a whisper remained, a gentle reminder
Of a love unrestrained, a love she never knew
A love that waited, through it all, for her to break through

Like a butterfly, she grew from cocoon to wings
Her spirit anew, emerging stronger, in Allah's gentle light
She rediscovered the love she'd forgotten, the love of Allah (SWT)
A love that's pure, true, and healing, that sees her through

Tears of joy and gratitude, she cries, for the love that's been
Her heart's reply, she weeps for the little girl, who once felt alone
But she rejoices, for the woman she's become, back home
In the depths of her soul, a spark now gleams, a sense of belonging

With Allah's love, she's found her peaceful nest, a sense of purpose
Every beat of her heart, every vessel that fills with blood
Every emotion, every experience, centred around Allah's love
She rises above pain, strives to fulfil His will, with every step

Through trials and tribulations, she stands firm and strong
A warrior, a survivor, a soul on fire, with a heart that beats for Allah (SWT)
A testament to faith, hope, and love's pure light
A shining star, guiding through the dark of night

With every step, she draws closer to His light
A journey of self-discovery, a path that's just right
She learns to trust, have faith, and abide
In the knowledge that Allah's love will be her guide

May Allah (SWT) guide us on our journey's path
Grant us wisdom to follow His gentle math
May His love and mercy surround us every day
And lead us to the truth, in a loving, gentle way
Ameen.

> "And indeed, My Mercy encompasses everything."
> (Quran 7:156)

Imagine being wrapped in a warm, golden light that knows no bounds – that's the mercy of Allah (SWT), encompassing every moment, every struggle, and every joy. His compassion is boundless. His benevolence is universal, and His love is infinite. May this truth bring you comfort, hope, and reassurance, reminding you that you are never beyond the reach of His mercy.

My Message to You
May this poem be a gentle breeze that soothes your soul, guiding you towards the warmth of Allah's love and mercy. May it inspire you to cultivate a deeper connection with our Rabb, and may your heart be filled with gratitude, peace, and joy. May Allah's presence be your solace, your strength, and your guiding light, illuminating your path with wisdom, love, and peace. Ameen.

PART 1
POEMS OF FAITH AND SPIRITUALITY
(WHISPERS OF THE DIVINE)

In Whispers of the Divine, I explore the depths of faith and spirituality, seeking guidance and connection with our Rabb.

Welcome to **Part 1** of my poetic journey,
"Poems of Faith and Spirituality."

As morning light whispers its gentle promise, the soul stirs, seeking connection with our beloved Rabb. Join me on this poetic journey, where faith and spirituality intertwine like delicate vines on a trellis, illuminating the path to inner peace, guidance, and healing.

Lessons Learnt and Takeaways
As you wander through these poems, may you discover hidden treasures that inspire you to:

1. **Surrender to Serenity:**
   Like a leaf on a tranquil stream, may our worries gently drift away, and may we find solace in the soothing whispers of the divine. **"And when My servants ask you,**

[O Muhammad], about Me - indeed I am near. I respond to the invocation of the supplicant when he calls upon Me." (Quran 2:186)

2. **Garden of Reflection:**
In the quiet hours of introspection, may we uncover the secrets of our own hearts, and may the seeds of growth and transformation take root. **"O you who have believed, fear Allah and let every soul consider what it has put forth for tomorrow - and fear Allah. Indeed, Allah is acquainted with what you do."** (Quran 59:18)

3. **Wings of Forgiveness:**
Like a bird set free, may forgiveness lift us above the burdens of resentment, and may compassion's gentle breeze soothe our souls. **"Let them pardon and forgive. Do you not love that Allah should forgive you?"** (Quran 24:22)

4. **Beacon of Hope:**
Through life's tempests, may we find the strength to weather every storm, and in the darkness, may a spark of hope illuminate the path forward. **"And indeed, with hardship comes ease."** (Quran 94:5)

5. **Blooming Love:**
Like a garden in full bloom, may our hearts overflow with love and kindness, nurturing the beauty of our humanity.

> **"And of His signs is that He created for you from yourselves mates that you may find tranquillity in them; and He placed between you affection and mercy."** (Quran 30:21)

May our journey be a divine journey, filled with peace, love, and a deeper connection with our Rabb. May our hearts be filled with wonder, awe, and gratitude, and may our lives be a reflection of the beauty and kindness that emanates from our souls. Ameen.

When darkness felt like a never-ending race, I found solace in the gentle whispers of my soul. This poem is a testament to the journey of spiritual growth, self-discovery, and devotion to Allah (SWT). May it guide you through life's challenges, reminding you to trust in His plan, cultivate humility, and find patience in His love. May His guidance illuminate your path, and may you find peace and joy in His divine presence...

"Echoes of the Soul"

Oh, beloved Rabb, hear my plea,
A heart that's seeking to be set free.
Forgive my past, and guide me anew,
Help me find patience and strength to see this through.

From time to time, I notice my old self appear,
A shadow of the past, a reminder to persevere.
But with Your guidance, I'll learn to let go,
And embrace the new me, with a heart that's aglow.

May my nafs fade, like a sunset's glow,
As humility's light begins to grow.
With every breath, I'll walk Your path,
Seeking guidance with a humble heart.

In Your mercy, I seek refuge and peace,
A sense of calm, my heart's release.
You are my treasure, my shining light,
My one true Rabb, my guiding sight.

Protect me from Shaytan's whispered lies,
And keep me steadfast, with a heart that sighs.
May my family join me in this journey of faith,
And may we together, find our way to Jannah's gate.

"And those who strive for Us - We will surely guide them to Our ways." (Quran 29:69)

Imagine being gently swept up in a warm breeze of guidance, carried toward the radiant light of Allah's love. This ayah whispers a promise of divine direction to those who strive for His pleasure, who take tender steps towards spiritual growth, and who nurture their soul with sincerity.

"The strong believer is better and more beloved to Allah than the weak believer, but there is good in each." (Sahih Muslim)

Let these words be a gentle nudge, encouraging you to bloom into the strongest, most vibrant version of yourself. May your heart be a garden of faith, nourished by patience, kindness, and love. May Allah's guidance be the sunshine that helps you grow, and may His mercy be the rain that quenches your soul.

My Message to You
May this poem be a soft whisper of inspiration, reminding you to reach out to Allah (SWT) in times of need, to trust in His boundless love and mercy, and to cultivate a deeper connection with the Divine. May His presence be your safe haven, your guiding star, and your soul's sanctuary. May you walk in the warmth of His love, and may His peace and joy be your constant companions. Ameen.

When life's path gets lost, and the way out seems far, that's when Allah's guidance shines like a star. Through whispers of our heart, He hears our call, offering love, mercy, and forgiveness, to one and all...

"Reach Out, for Allah (SWT) is Near"

Reach out for Allah (SWT) is near; He knows your struggles, your deepest fear.
No matter the burden, no matter the test,
Reach out, for He waits to hear your heartfelt quest.

In the depths of your soul, where shadows roam,
Reach out to Allah and call Him your own.
He knows the whispers of your heart, the tears you've cried,
And in His mercy, your struggles will be denied.

With every breath, with every beat,
He is near, a love so sweet.
Don't let Shaytan's whispers deceive,
You are worthy; you are loved; and you are believed.

He knows the battles you face, the trials you endure,
For He placed them in your path, to strengthen your faith, to ensure.
Stay firm, stay strong; reach out to your Lord,
The King of Kings, Majesty Supreme, His mercy, love, and forgiveness, He freely brings.
He is the King of Kings, the Majesty Supreme,

Your Creator, your Guide, your Heart's Esteem.
Reach out to Him, with hands open wide,
And let His love, mercy, and forgiveness be your guide.
In the darkness, He is the light.
In the silence, He is the sound of delight.
He knows your truth; He knows your name,
And with His love, you'll never feel ashamed.

So reach out to Him, with a heart so true,
And let His mercy envelop me and you.
For in His love, we find our peace,
A love that's pure, a love that never will cease.

What waits is beyond compare, a treasure to behold,
For His love, mercy, and forgiveness are worth more than gold.
He knows the truth within. He knows you better than you know,
He is your Creator, your Supreme; reach out to Him, and let your spirit glow.

May Allah's love be the guiding light,
In your heart, in your soul, shining so bright.
May you feel His presence in every single way,
And may His mercy be with you, every step of the day.

Ameen.

"And when My servants ask you, [O Muhammad], about Me – indeed I am near. I respond to the invocation of the supplicant when he calls upon Me. So let them respond to Me [by obedience] and believe in Me – that they may be [rightly] guided." (Quran 2:186)

Imagine being wrapped in the warmth of Allah's presence, where every whisper, every prayer, and every heartbeat is heard and responded to. This ayah reminds us that Allah (SWT) is always near, always listening, and always guiding us toward the light. May we find comfort in His nearness, peace in His response, and guidance in His wisdom.

My Message to You
May this poem be a gentle reminder of the power of prayer and the nearness of Allah's love. May it inspire you to reach out to Him in times of need, to trust in His mercy and forgiveness, and to cultivate a deeper sense of faith and connection with the Divine. May Allah's presence be your sanctuary, your guiding light, and your soul's haven. May you walk in the peace and joy of His divine presence, now and always. Ameen.

With tender hearts and seeking souls, we reach out to our Rabb. In the quiet moments, our deepest duas unfold... This is one such dua that saw me through life's trials, when self-doubt whispered low, and hope needed a gentle glow...

"Ya Rabb, My Beloved Rabb"

Ya Rabb, my beloved Rabb,
There have been so many lessons that have come my way.
Sometimes I see glimpses of who I used to be.
Forgive me, my beloved, oh so Supreme.

I don't like that version, nor do I favour her much.
I ask for Your assistance to groom her, to help her grow and flourish.
Let her take control of her nafs (ego), so she may disappear and continue to grow.
Help her find
her peace,
calm, and
complete
delight.

Oh, my beloved Rabb, I ask with humility, for You know what's best.
Know it takes time to grow and evolve; may You please help me.
Oh, may You please help me, my Rabb, to find patience and strength from above.

I look forward to the days when I can say, "Oh, how silly I was along the way."

To be happy and whole, forever and a day.
I know that this is a big ask, my beloved Rabb.
May I continue to walk on Your path, finding delight and greatness,
until I meet You at Jannah's gate.

Ameen.

"And indeed, with hardship comes ease." (Quran 94:5)

Imagine a gentle dawn breaking after a long night, symbolising the promise of relief and comfort that follows every hardship. This ayah reminds us that challenges are temporary, but Allah's mercy and guidance are constant. May we find strength in patience, solace in prayer, and ease in His divine presence.

My Message to You
May this poem be a beacon of hope, inspiring you to cultivate humility, self-awareness, and perseverance on your spiritual journey. May it guide you to recognise your shortcomings and work towards growth, seeking Allah's guidance and support every step of the way. May His love and mercy envelop you, bringing

peace and joy to your heart. May you walk in the light of His guidance, finding ease and comfort in His divine presence. Ameen.

The Adhan's gentle melody drifts through the air, our hearts are stirred, and our souls are reminded of our Rabb's loving presence. In its haunting beauty, we find solace, guidance, and a call to the heart's deepest longing...

"The Call to Prayer"

In the symphony of life, the call to prayer resonates,
A celestial melody that echoes Allah's loving states,
A reminder to breathe, to pause, to reflect and adore,
The beauty of faith that guides us, and so much more.

With every echo, my heart beats faster; my soul feels alive,
A sense of connection to something greater, I thrive.
The call to prayer, a blessing, a gift from above,
A reminder of Allah's love, a labour of love.

How blessed are we to hear the call to prayer,
A constant reminder that Allah (SWT) is near.
From meadows, through valleys, and cities ablaze,
The call to prayer echoes aloud, in praise.

What once felt like a chore now sounds like delight,
A place to look forward to, where love shines so bright.
A space filled with devotion, where hearts beat as one,
In praise of our Creator, our Supreme, our Beloved One.

I cherish the call to prayer that echoes through the day
A reminder to give thanks, to seek guidance along the way.
To share my successes and ask for strength in times of strife,
To seek protection, love, and mercy from our Rabb, our Creator, our Life.

Oh, how I love the sounds of prayer that echo through the earth,
A treasure so precious, a gift of infinite worth.
Some may see it as an irritation, but to me, it's life itself,
A reminder of Allah's presence, a blessing, a gift, a wealth.

Who is blessed, you who despise it, or me who holds it dear?
I'll cherish the call to prayer and hold it close, year after year.
For in its echoes, I hear the voice of my Beloved One,
Guiding me, protecting me, until we meet, beneath the throne.

In the stillness of dawn, in the heat of the day,
In the quiet of the night, the call to prayer finds its way.

"And indeed, with hardship comes ease." (Quran 94:5)

Imagine the Adhan's gentle call, a soothing melody that brings comfort and peace to the soul. This ayah reminds us that even in challenging times, ease and relief are on the horizon. May the Adhan be a beacon of hope, guiding you towards Allah's love and presence, and may its beauty and significance inspire deeper devotion and connection.

My Message to You

May this poem be a heartfelt reminder of the Adhan's power to soothe, guide, and uplift. May its call to prayer awaken your spirit, reminding you of Allah's love, mercy, and presence in your life. May you find comfort, peace, and joy in the Adhan's melody, and may it inspire you to cultivate a deeper sense of spirituality and devotion. May Allah's love and guidance be your constant companion, now and always. Ameen.

Amidst life's whirlwind, a gentle whisper beckons: breathe, reflect, and find peace. In the stillness, our souls awaken, and our hearts reconnect with our Rabb...

Ameen.

"Find Your Calm Spirit"

In a world that's busy, loud and wide,
Find your calm spirit, where love resides.
A place of serenity, where hearts can roam,
Free to be yourself, in your authentic home.

It's where the noise subsides, and peace takes hold,
Your soul revives, and your heart unfolds.
No pretences needed, no masks to wear,
Just the purest version of the person you are.

As the Quran reminds us, "And indeed, with hardship comes ease." (94:5)
Find solace in prayer and the words of Allah's peace.
In the stillness of night, or the quiet of dawn,
Connect with your Lord, and let your heart be reborn.

So nourish your soul with moments of calm.
Find your peaceful haven, where love is the balm.
For in being your authentic self, you'll find,
The greatest gift of all, a heart and soul aligned.

May Allah (SWT) guide us to our calm spirit's place,
Where love, peace, and serenity fill every space.

"**And indeed, with hardship comes ease.**" (Quran 94:5)

Imagine a calm oasis in the midst of life's storms, where peace and serenity bloom. This ayah reminds us that even in hardship, ease is forthcoming. May we find solace in Allah's presence, cultivating spiritual well-being through prayer, reflection, and stillness. May our hearts be aligned with peace, serenity, and love.

My Message to You
May this poem be a gentle guide, inspiring you to prioritise your spiritual well-being and seek calm in chaos. May it remind you to connect with Allah (SWT) through prayer and reflection, finding authenticity and peace in quiet moments. May your heart be filled with serenity, love, and peace, and may your soul be aligned with His divine guidance. May Allah's peace and love envelop you, now and always. Ameen.

Like stars shining bright in the night sky, our unique paths unfold, guided by the light of faith and the whispers of our hearts. A reflection on the beauty of individuality and the strength of spiritual devotion....

"You Do You and I'll Do Me"

In a world of chaos, where desires roar loudly,
I've found solace in Allah's love, and a heart that adores.
The fleeting dreams of vanity no longer hold me tight,
For I've discovered a treasure that shines with divine light.

Celebrities, once idols, now mere mortals to me,
Their fame and fortune no longer a fantasy,
For Allah (SWT), Most High, the King of Kings, my Supreme,
Is the only one worthy of my heart's esteem.

My heart beats for the beauty of Hijab's gentle fold,
A symbol of modesty, and a soul that's made of gold.
The Quran's melody and Naseeb's gentle sway,
Fill my heart with joy and light the way.

Fast cars and big houses no longer hold allure,
For I've found a home in Allah (SWT) love, and a heart that's pure.
My haven of love, joy, and laughter is where I reside,
A place where His glare lights the way, and is my guide.

You do you, and I'll do me,

Two paths, two choices, eternity to see.
Who's the best one? I ask, with a humble heart,
Is it you, or is it me? Only Allah (SWT) knows from the start.
So let's walk our paths, with faith and love in tow,
And let His glare light the way, as we go.
May our choices lead us to eternity's gate,
Where love, joy, and peace, forever await.

May Allah (SWT) guide us on our journey through life,
and fill our hearts with love and a deep, inner light.
May we always remember that He's always near,
And that His love and guidance dispel all fear.

"Indeed, this is My straight path, so follow it; and do not follow [other] paths, for they will separate you from His way." (Quran 6:153)

Imagine walking on a radiant path, illuminated by the light of Allah's guidance. This ayah reminds us to stay true to our faith, prioritising our relationship with Allah (SWT) above all else. May we follow His path with confidence, avoiding the distractions of worldly temptations, and may His love and light guide us every step of the way.

My Message to You

May this poem be a beacon of guidance, inspiring you to stay true to your faith and values. May it remind you to prioritise your relationship with Allah (SWT), following His path with confidence and conviction. May His love and light illuminate your journey, guiding you towards eternity's gate, where love, joy, and peace await. May Allah's guidance and mercy be your constant companion, now and forever. Ameen.

Beware the whispers of the shadows, for in the silence, choices are made. Let wisdom guide our steps, and faith illuminate our path, as we navigate life's journey with purpose and heart...

"Beware of Shaytan's Whispers"

Oh, dear soul, beware of Shaytan's call,
A whispered deceit that beckons you to fall,
He preys on your emotions and feeds on your pain,
A merciless enemy, with no love to gain.

Foolish are we to choose him time and again,
Ignoring the warning signs and the eternal pain,
His fleeting pleasures, a moment's delight,
But the consequences of our choices will haunt us through the night.

Oh, dear heart, be very, very afraid,
For the Day of Reckoning draws near, and your deeds will be displayed,
Two angels as witnesses to all that you've done,
The good and the bad, even the deeds you've forgotten, one by one.

Which path will you choose, dear soul, which way will you stray?
Will it be the path of righteousness, or the road to dismay?
The choice is yours, but oh, the consequences are real,

Allah's pleasure or wrath awaits, and your soul will reveal.

So heed the warning, dear heart, and beware of Shaytan's snare,
For on the Day of Judgement, there's no one to blame but yourself; you'll bear,
The weight of your deeds, the choices you've made,
Oh, dear soul, choose wisely, and fear Allah (SWT), before it's too late.

May Allah (SWT) guide us and protect us from the evil one,
May He grant us wisdom and the strength to have won,
The battle against our ego and the whispers of Shaytan's might,
May we choose the path of righteousness and shine with Allah's light.

"Oh you who have believed, enter into Islam completely, tend perfectly, and do not follow the footsteps of Satan. Indeed, he is to you a clear enemy." (Quran 2:208)

Imagine standing strong on the path of righteousness, illuminated by the light of faith and guided by Allah's wisdom. This ayah reminds us to be vigilant against Shaytan's whispers, making choices that align with our values and faith. May we cultivate spiritual strength and wisdom, avoiding the path of sin and following the guidance of Allah (SWT).

My Message to You

May this poem be a powerful reminder to be mindful of Shaytan's influence and to strive for righteousness. May it inspire you to make choices that please Allah (SWT), cultivating spiritual strength and wisdom in your journey. May Allah (SWT) guide and protect you from the evil one, granting you the wisdom and strength to walk the path of righteousness. May His mercy and love envelop you, now and always. Ameen.

In the whispers of the wind, the rustle of leaves, and the twinkle of stars, we find the fingerprints of our Rabb. A tribute to the Majesty that surrounds us, guides us, and loves us beyond measure...

"I See You, Oh Allah (SWT)"

In the depths of my soul, I see You, oh Allah (SWT), so divine,
A reflection of Your majesty, in every heartbeat, every breath of mine.
You are the Creator of all, the Source of every life,
In Your wisdom, I find solace, my heart's eternal strife.

I see You in the miracle of existence, in every atom, every cell,
A masterpiece of Your craftsmanship, a symphony that echoes so well.
In the vast expanse of the universe, I see Your handiwork so grand,
A celestial tapestry, woven with threads of Your divine command.

I see You in every grain of sand, every desert, and across the land,
In every leaf that falls, in every branch and root that grows, so planned.
I see You in the majesty of mountains, where even the tallest peaks can't reach Your throne,
I see You in the depths of the ocean, in every fish, every sea creature, and mystery below.

I see You in every sunrise; Your divine light shining bright,
Illuminating paths, guiding us through life's journey, day and night.
I see You in every sunset, in the winds that blow,
Your mighty force that shapes the world below.

I see You in every drop of rain, in lightning's flash, in thunder's roar,
Reminding me of Your power, Your majesty, forever in store.
I see You when day turns to night, in darkness and in light,
A reminder to rest, to reflect, and be thankful for Your guidance and might.

Oh, Allah (SWT), Oh so supreme, what have I to lose or gain?
You are the essence of every breath, the heartbeat of every vein.
You are my Lord, my everything, my heart beats for You alone,
In Your presence, I am humbled, my soul forever made known.

You are my Lord, my everything, my guiding light, my way.
I long to be with You, in Jannah's gardens, on Judgment Day.
I yearn to see Your face, to gaze upon Your divine glory,
To hear Your voice, saying "Enter, My servant, into My mercy."

I see You in every moment, in every breath, in every sigh,
A constant reminder of Your love, Your mercy, passing me by.
May I forever see You, Oh Allah (SWT), in every moment, every breath,

May my heart remain pure, my soul forever in Your depths.
May I walk in Your light, guided by Your love and might.

Forever humbled, forever grateful, in Your presence.
Oh Allah (SWT), my sight.
I can't wait to see You at Jannah's gate,
Where love, peace, and joy await, and my heart will forever celebrate.

"Wherever you turn, there is the face of Allah." (Quran 2:115)

Imagine being surrounded by the infinite presence of Allah (SWT), where every moment, every breath, and every glance reveals His majesty. This ayah reminds us that He is all-encompassing, aware of everything, and present everywhere. May we cultivate a deeper sense of awareness and connection with Allah (SWT), recognising His presence in every aspect of creation.

My Message to You

May this poem be a gentle reminder of Allah's omnipresent love and guidance. May it inspire you to walk in His light, remaining humble, grateful, and pure in His presence. May your heart be filled with the awareness of His majesty, and may you be guided by His love and might in every step of your journey. May Allah's presence be your comfort, peace, and strength, now and forever. Ameen.

As We Conclude Part 1

As the morning light of **Part 1, "Poems of Faith and Spirituality,"** gently fades, may the whispers of these words linger in your heart like a soft breeze that carries the scent of rose petals. May the lessons learnt and reflections sparked by these poems guide you towards a deeper connection with our Rabb, illuminating your path with the gentle glow of purpose, compassion, and kindness.

May our souls be nurtured by the words of Allah (SWT) and the teachings of Prophet Muhammad (PBUH), like a garden that blooms in the warm light of faith. May our hearts overflow with love, kindness, and peace, like a fountain that flows with gentle tranquillity.

As we embark on **Part 2, "Poems of Love and Connection,"** join me on this enchanting journey of exploring the beauty and complexity of human relationships. May these poems ignite reflections on your own relationships, nurturing love, kindness, and compassion in your heart like a warm ember that glows with gentle light.

May Allah (SWT) bless us with:

- Hearts that dance with love and kindness
- Minds that shine with understanding and empathy
- Spirits that soar with peace and harmony

May our poetic journey be a source of inspiration, guidance, and joy, illuminating our paths toward healing, growth, and transformation. Ameen.

PART 2

POEMS OF LOVE AND CONNECTION
(TIES THAT BIND)

In Ties That Bind, I celebrate the beauty of family bonds, love, and relationships, honouring the ones who bring joy and strength to our lives.

Welcome to **Part 2** of my poetic journey,
"Love and Connection"

As love and connection wrap their tender threads around our hearts, the soul stirs, yearning for deeper bonds with family and friends. Join me on this poetic adventure, where love and family ties bloom like a whimsical garden of roses, filling our lives with warmth, laughter, and joy. May these poems be the gentle breeze that whispers sweet nothings to your heart, inspiring you to nurture relationships that bring love, peace, and happiness to your life.

Lessons Learnt and Takeaways
As you wander through these poems, may you discover hidden treasures that inspire you to :

1. **Garden of Family Love:**
   In the garden of love, may our hearts bloom with kindness, patience, and understanding, just as the wisest of guides taught us to tend to our loved ones with gentle care. **"The best of you are those who are best to their families."** (Hadith, Narrated by Ibn Majah)

2. **Bouquet of Gratitude:**
   May our hearts overflow with thankfulness for the precious gifts of family and friends, and may we treasure every moment, every laugh, and every tear. **"Whatever blessings you have, they are from Allah."** (Quran 16:53)

3. **Tapestry of Meaningful Relationships:**
   Like a bouquet of flowers, may our friendships and community ties bring joy and beauty to our lives, and may we surround ourselves with kindred spirits who inspire us to grow. **"A person is on the religion of his close friend, so let each of you look to who he takes as a close friend."** (Hadith, Narrated by Abu Dawud)

4. **Heartfelt Compassion:**
   May our relationships be a reflection of the beauty and kindness that radiates from our hearts, and may we show compassion to those around us. **"The One in the heavens will show compassion to you."** (Hadith Qudsi, Narrated by Abu Dawud)

5. **Rope of Unity:**
   Like a tapestry of love, may our relationships be strengthened by the threads of Islamic values, and may we build strong, resilient bonds with those around us. "**And hold firmly to the rope of Allah all together and do not become divided**" (Quran 3:103).

May our journey be a whimsical dance, filled with warmth, laughter, and joy, and may our hearts be filled with love, kindness, and connection. May our relationships be a source of strength, comfort, and inspiration, and may we emerge from this journey with hearts full of love, compassion, and peace. Ameen.

Testament to the beauty of relationships that flourish through laughter, tears, and shared moments. Here's a heartfelt tribute to the ones who make our lives richer...

"Threads of Love"

In life's tapestry, we're threads of love,
Woven together, sent from above.
My husband, my rock, my guiding light,
My partner through life's darkest night.

You're the sunshine that brightens my day,
And lights up the night, in every way.
Your laughter, smiles, hugs, and tears,
Are memories I treasure, through all the passing years.

Our children, precious jewels bright,
Laughter, tears, and memories through day and night.
You've grown with every step, with every fall,
With every rise, our love for you multiplies, one and all.

Our daughter-in-law, a treasure,
Bringing joy, love, and goodness anew.
You've enriched our family with your presence so fine,
A gift from Allah (SWT), a treasure we cherish, all the time.

Our granddaughters, sweet blossoms in our lives,
Filling hearts with delight, and joyful, contagious giggles that thrive.
You're the melody that fills our hearts,

The sweetness that makes us whole, a love that never departs.

Together we've stood, through trials and tests,
Our love the sun that never rests.
Shukran, Ya Rabb, for this gift divine,
A family's love, a treasure so fine.

May Allah (SWT) guide us, forgive our sins,
And grant us Jannah's bliss within.
May we meet at Jannah's gate,
In eternal peace and love, forevermore,
Ameen.

"And we have honoured the children of Adam." (Quran 17:70)

Imagine being wrapped in the warmth of Allah's love and honour, cherished as a precious creation. This ayah reminds us of the inherent value and dignity of every individual, highlighting the importance of kindness, compassion, and respect. May we cherish and appreciate the blessings of loved ones, recognising the beauty and joy they bring to our lives.

My Message to You

May this poem be a heartfelt reminder to appreciate the gift of family and loved ones. May it inspire you to express gratitude for their presence in your life and seek Allah's blessings and guidance for them. May your family be filled with love, peace, and happiness, and may Allah's mercy and care surround them always. May His blessings be upon you and your loved ones, now and forever. Ameen.

Like rose petals that leave their fragrance on the hands that give them, mothers leave their love, wisdom, and legacy on the hearts they touch. A heartfelt tribute to the selfless love and sacrifices of our mothers, and the power of breaking cycles to forge a brighter future...

"Our Dearest Treasures, Our Loving Mums"

You endured life's difficulties with strength and might,
Striving to give us the best, though you didn't have it in sight.
Sometimes forgetting it was love that we seemed to need,
You showed us love in your own way, though it wasn't always easy to read.

We now understand it was your way to make up for what went wrong.
Though you didn't receive love's spell, your love for us remained strong.
No matter what, our dear mums, we love and treasure you still,
Cherishing sweet memories, your delightful treats, and thoughtful gifts that fulfil.

We forgive and treasure those moments, dear loving mums of ours,
Gifts from Almighty Allah (SWT) above, who knows you did your best with what you had in store.
Years later, wiser and more loving, we miss our chats and even our fights,
Working hard to break generational patterns that our children may feel loved and whole, shining with delight.

That they may understand, as we now do, that bad habits take time to undo,
We're on our way to doing what's right, that our children may feel our love, pure and true.
You're our mothers, our hearts' delight, chosen by Allah (SWT) for us to treasure and hold tight.

Though you may be gone, your memory stays near,
Missing you with every heartbeat, we hold you dear.
With Allah's love, we know we'll be alright,
Guided by His light, shining through the darkest night.

May peace be upon you, dear mothers, wherever you may be,
May Allah (SWT) forgive us for our sins and lighten our paths, that we may meet again, wild and free.
At Jannah's gate, with open arms, we'll welcome you with love,
Grateful for Allah's lessons, which brought us full circle, sent from above.

"And we have enjoined upon man [to be good] to his parents. His mother carried him, [increasing her in weakness upon weakness, and his weaning is in two years. Be grateful to Me and to your parents; to Me is the [final] destination." (Quran 31:14)

Imagine the selfless love of a mother, carrying her child with strength and devotion, and the sacrifices of parents who nurture and guide. This ayah reminds us to show gratitude and respect to our parents, thanking Allah (SWT) for the gift of family. May we appreciate their love and sacrifices, recognising the value of forgiveness, healing, and growth.

My Message to You
May this poem be a heartfelt tribute to the love and devotion of mothers and parents. May it inspire you to cherish their sacrifices, seek forgiveness, and break free from past patterns. May you strive to create a brighter future for yourself and your loved ones, filled with love, peace, and happiness. May Allah (SWT) bless your family with His mercy and care, guiding you towards a path of gratitude, love, and harmony. Ameen.

Sisters in soul, bound by love and life's intricate threads, our bond weaves a tale of forgiveness, strength, and tender care. A heartfelt ode to the beauty of relationships, where faith and compassion guide us through life's trials, and love becomes the bridge that heals and unites...

"A Sister's Love"

A sister, a treasure, a gift from above,
Not bound by blood, but a bond of endless love.
You've been a rock, a guiding light,
A source of strength in the darkest night.

But I see the pain, the hurt you've faced,
Consuming your heart, a weight you've placed.
Struggling to face the traumas of the past,
Filtering down to loved ones, it's time to look vast.

"Indeed, with hardship comes ease." (Quran 94:5)
Let's find solace in this promise and strive to release,
The chains that bind us, the pain we've known,
And find peace, forgiveness, and love that's shown.

Prophet Muhammad taught, "The strong believer is better and more beloved to Allah than the weak believer." (Sahih Muslim)

Let's find strength in our faith and in each other,
And learn to let go, to forgive, and to smother,
The hurt and pain, and be the person we know,
A person of love, care, and light, as we grow.

You're a sister, a friend, a mother, beyond compare,
A treasure, a blessing, a gift so rare.
May Allah (SWT) guide you as you move on,
To being the person we know you're meant to be, strong.

Let's take a lesson from the Quran, "And let them pardon and overlook.
Would you not like that Allah should forgive you?" (Quran 24:22)
Let's pardon, overlook, and forgive,
And find peace, love, and light in our lives, and live.

"And let them pardon and overlook. Would you not like that Allah should forgive you?" (Quran 24:22)

Imagine the liberating power of forgiveness, where hearts are lightened and relationships are healed. This ayah reminds us to pardon others and overlook their mistakes, just as Allah (SWT) forgives us. May we cultivate compassion, empathy, and love, promoting peace and unity in our relationships.

My Message to You
May this poem be a gentle reminder of the transformative power of forgiveness and love. May it inspire you to reflect on the importance of empathy and compassion in your relationships, finding strength in your faith and the bonds of love that unite you.

May you uplift and support each other on your journey towards personal growth and spiritual enlightenment. May Allah's mercy and forgiveness guide you, filling your heart with love, peace, and harmony. Ameen.

A bond of sisterhood, woven with threads of love, laughter, and tender moments, a treasure trove of memories and heartfelt emotions. A heartfelt tribute to the selfless love, unwavering strength, and kindness of a sister, a shining star that brightens life's journey...

"Oh Sister, Oh Sister"

Oh sister, oh sister, blood of mine,
Oh, how much you mean to me, you will never understand.
Being like a mum to me since my teenage years into adulthood,
Always there to lend me a helping hand.

Trials and turbulations cannot keep us apart,
All it does is bring us closer in heart.
Oh sister, oh sister, blood of mine,
Seeing how you share your love has been divine.

Selfless and caring, oh so kind,
How I love seeing this side of you.
Could not quite understand why you do the things you do,
Even when others treat you badly, you never shy away.

I see how they hurt you, and it tears me apart,
Sometimes I just feel like screaming at them for what they do.
And I know it's not my place, for this is your journey to see it through.
Know that I love you very much, and Allah (SWT) sees all that you put up with, and your reward is greater than this life's worth.

I see how you take care of our brothers at large; know that you are my shining star.

I am not always there to give you a hand, and I am thankful that you understand.
I treasure our monthly sister time together, sharing all our troubles, successes, and love.

Oh sister, how I love you; this you surely know,
For I tell you this constantly, which I never used to do.
May Allah's blessings always be with you,
Please keep at what you're doing, and never change; you are blessed beyond measure, and I am pleased for you.

May your path to Jannah be easy,
I can't wait to meet you at Jannah's gate and the beyond,
so we may continue to keep our flame alive.
I love you, dear sister, forevermore, kind.

Ameen.

"And those who believe and do righteous deeds - We will surely give them a high rank among the righteous." (Quran 4:69)

Imagine the joy of living a life filled with purpose and virtue, where good deeds and faith guide every step. This ayah reassures us that our righteous actions will be recognised and rewarded by Allah (SWT), granting us a high rank among the righteous. May we cherish love, kindness, and compassion, and strive to live a life that pleases Him.

My Message to You

May this poem be a reminder of the value of living a virtuous life and doing good deeds. May it inspire you to cultivate kindness, compassion, and selflessness, appreciating the special relationships in your life. May you strive to please Allah (SWT) in all that you do, and may your good actions be rewarded with a high rank among the righteous. May His mercy and blessings be upon you, guiding you towards a life of purpose and virtue. Ameen.

Like rays of sunshine that brighten our days, true friends illuminate our lives with love, laughter, and unwavering support. A heartfelt ode to the precious gift of friendship, celebrating the bonds that uplift, inspire, and bring joy to our journey...

"Friends: Rare Gems from Above"

Rare gems, precious friends, sent from above,
True companions, who show us enduring love.
Unafraid to speak the truth, with words that heal and mend,
Reminding us to align our actions with our heart's intent.

In the tapestry of life, you are the threads of gold,
Woven into the fabric of our hearts, forever to hold.
True friends, precious gems, sent from Allah's loving hand,
A treasure to cherish, a blessing to stand.

You are the constant reminders that we're not alone in our care,
Your presence is a gift, a treasure to behold, polishing and shining us when our spirits grow old.
A safe haven where we can be our true selves,
A sanctuary of trust, where our hearts can find their wealth.

May Allah (SWT) guide us to cherish and honour friends like you,
And may we strive to be the same blessing to them, too.
May our paths be filled with meaningful connections and love,
Walking together under Allah's guidance, sent from above.

May Allah (SWT) strengthen our bond and deepen our connection,
May our friendship be a source of inspiration and affection.
May we continue to uplift and support each other's way,
And may our love and loyalty be a shining light each day.

In a world that can be uncertain, you are the constant we adore,
A reminder that we're not alone, that we have each other, and more.
So here's to our friendship, a treasure we hold dear,
A blessing from Allah (SWT) that brings us joy and wipes away our tears.

"And the believers, men and women, are protecting friends one of another; they enjoin the right and forbid the wrong..." (Quran 9:71)

Imagine the warmth of supportive friendships, where believers uplift and guide each other towards righteousness. This ayah reminds us to cherish and nurture meaningful relationships, built on mutual support and a shared commitment to doing good. May our friendships be a source of strength, inspiration, and love, reflecting the values of compassion, empathy, and kindness.

My Message to You
May this poem be a celebration of the beauty and value of supportive friendships. May it inspire you to nurture your relationships, seeking Allah's guidance to strengthen bonds of friendship and promote righteousness. May your friendships be a source of joy, comfort, and love, and may you be a source of inspiration and support for one another. May Allah's blessings and mercy be upon your friendships, now and forever. Ameen.

A life well-lived leaves an indelible mark on hearts and memories, and though seasons change, the warmth of love remains. A heartfelt tribute to my beloved brother-in-law, a guiding light whose legacy of love, wisdom, and kindness continues to inspire and uplift, forever cherished in our hearts...

"A Guardian Angel, Sent From Above"

Oh, brother-in-law of mine, sent from above,
A guardian angel, a labour of love.
You were the pillar of our family's might,
A shining example, guiding us through life's plight.

With love and care, you took me in as your own,
A father figure, forever in my heart, forever home.
Your unwavering love stood the test of time,
Through laughter and tears, you were always on my mind.

You taught me to stand tall, to face every test,
A true example of what a father should be, you did your best.
I cherish the memories of our Sunday meals prep,
Washing your car for extra pocket money, a privilege to step.

Into your world, where love and discipline entwined,
Shaping me into the person I am today, forever aligned.
Your phone calls, a surprise, a delight,
Checking in, showing love, a father's guiding light.

You treated my sister, nieces with love and care,
A true guardian, leaving a legacy beyond compare.
Tough at times, but with our best interests at heart,

We understand now and never will depart.

From the values you taught, the love you showed,
Forever in our hearts, a love that will forever glow.
Rest in peace, dear brother-in-law of mine,
May Allah (SWT) ease your journey, until we meet at Jannah's gate divine.

We miss you dearly, but your memory stays near,
A blessing, a treasure, a love that casts out fear.

"And We have certainly honoured the children of Adam."
(Quran 17:70)

Imagine the profound impact of kindness, compassion, and love on the lives of those around us. This ayah reminds us of the inherent value and dignity of every human being, highlighting the importance of treating others with respect and empathy. May we cherish the time we have with loved ones, striving to make a positive difference in the world.

My Message to You
May this poem be a heartfelt reminder to appreciate the people in your life and to live with purpose. May it inspire you to spread kindness, compassion, and love, leaving a lasting impact on those

around you. May you be guided by the values of empathy and respect, honouring the memories of loved ones by living a life that makes a difference. May Allah's mercy and blessings be upon you, inspiring you to touch the lives of others with love and kindness. Ameen.

Brotherhood is a tapestry woven with threads of laughter, tears, and shared moments, each strand telling a story of love, struggle, and resilience. A heartfelt ode to the bonds that tie us, this tribute weaves together threads of empathy, understanding, and devotion, seeking guidance and peace for each of my brothers' journey...

"Brothers of Blood"

My eldest brother, I see your pain,
A soul wounded deep, with scars that remain.
Lost your sight, like a sunset in the night,
A darkness that surrounds, a challenge to ignite.
The spark within you, that once shone so bright,
May Allah guide you, through this darkest of nights.
May you find peace and solace, and let go of the past.
Trust in our Rabb, for He knows what's best at last.
You lost your family, something I will not understand anew.
We don't know the What?, Why? or How? it came to be.
Your refusal to tell us leaves us with uncertainty.
May Allah (SWT) guide you through this trial and strife,
And grant you peace and solace in His life.

My second eldest brother, gone too soon,
I barely knew you, but memories remain
Athletic star, trophies won,
Potential unfulfilled, yet the spirit shone.
.Your struggles, a heart of gold,
A beggar in life but rich in spirit, never to grow old.
I miss our conversations, your surprise visits so dear,
Memories imprinted in my heart, always near.
I believe you're happy now, in a better place,
May our Rabb reward you for the trials you faced.

My third eldest brother, losing your first wife was a blow,
Four children to care for, with a heart that was low.
You started a family anew, with step-children and two additional daughters too,
And you've walked this path, with challenges anew.
Yet, some children strayed, neglected and apart,
May Allah (SWT) mend your relationships and heal your heart.

My fourth eldest brother, gone too soon, you lost your wife,
And struggled with depression; we didn't know until too late, too soon.
Your laughter echoes still, your pride and joy,
You tried to stay in touch with your children, which was sometimes challenging.
I guess we'll never know why you chose to end your life.
But your passing left us shocked, with tears to employ.
I was upset, angry, and hurt by the choice you made,
A sin, I knew, but judgment is for our Rabb to convey.
I've learnt that I cannot place judgment on you,
Forgive me, dear brother, for being angry at you.

My last-born brother, with a heart of gold,
Chosen to care for us, a role you've been told.
You neglected your duty, as a father, I know,
But I pray our Rabb mends your relationship, and makes it grow.
Mend your relationships, enjoy the time you have left,
Live your life with happiness, and find peace, find rest.

I believe in you, dear brother, you can do better, you can try.
For the sake of your daughter and your own soul, don't ask why?

To all my brothers, I may not always be there,
As our sister is there for you.
But when you reach out, know that I am here for you too,
A sister's love, a bond that's strong, forever true.
May Allah (SWT) bless you and keep you safe,
And grant you peace, and love that's not a mistake.
Brothers of blood, bound by love and fate,
May our bond remain strong, despite life's weight.

"And hold firmly to the rope of Allah all together and do not become divided." (Quran 3:103)

Imagine the strength of unity and cohesion among believers, where hearts are connected and minds are aligned. This ayah reminds us to hold fast to our faith and to each other, navigating life's challenges with empathy, understanding, and support. May our bond with Allah (SWT) and with one another be the foundation of our resilience and peace.

My Message to You

This poem weaves a tale of love and connection, highlighting the tender threads that bind us together as family and believers. It's a reminder that sibling bonds are a precious gift, and that empathy, understanding, and support are the soft whispers that nurture meaningful relationships. When challenges arise, faith and forgiveness become the guiding lights that lead us through the darkness, and unity and cohesion among believers are the strong foundations that hold us fast.

May this poem be a gentle breeze that carries the fragrance of love and connection into your heart. May it inspire you to tend to your relationships with kindness, compassion, and empathy, and to seek Allah's guidance and support in times of need. May you be reminded of the transformative power of forgiveness and understanding, and may your relationships be a reflection of the beauty and love that binds us together. Ameen.

A father's absence leaves an unspoken silence, yet in its depths, a journey of self-discovery and spiritual growth unfolds. A heartfelt exploration of pain, forgiveness, and healing, guided by the unwavering love and mercy of our Rabb, who fills the voids of the past with the light of His presence...

"A Message to My Father"

In title alone, you held the name,
A father's love, I never knew, the pain.
Abandoned at four or five, I remained,
A childhood scarred, a heart in pain.

Yet, a memory lingered, a glimpse of the past,
Standing on the back seat, wind blowing fast.
A trip to the sweet factory shop, a treat so fine,
A moment with you, forever etched in my mind.

Years went by, and I wondered if it was true,
A dream, perhaps, born of longing and missing you.
But then I discovered it was real, a memory so bright,
You took me to the sweet shop, a fleeting moment of delight.

My subconscious held on, a testament to the pain,
A heart that longed for a father's love, in vain.
Growing up without you, surrounded by friends with dads,
I wished you were there, but now I understand the reasons you had.

Mum never spoke ill of you; her love for you remained,
A silence that spoke volumes, a heart that still felt the pain.
The scars you left behind, a legacy of hurt and strife,

Affected each of us, a pain that cut deep, a wound that wouldn't heal in life.

Some of my siblings followed in your footsteps, it's true,
Absent in their own children's lives, a cycle of pain, anew.
But I've made peace with the past, forgiven the hurt and the pain,
Understood that you did the best you could, with the resources you had gained.

I forgive you, father dear, though I'll never call you dad,
Someone else filled that spot, a love that made me feel less sad.
Allah (SWT) sent me guidance angels, three strong men who loved me truly,
My husband, son, and brother-in-law, a love that shines, pure, and new.

Above all, I've learnt that the One who loved me most,
Was always beside me, guiding me through every test.
"Al Wahid", my Saviour, the One who set me free,
A love that's unconditional, a heart that's full, and a soul that's me.

Alhamdulillah, Subhanallah, Allah-u-Akbar,
I praise Him, I glorify Him, Allah (SWT) is the Greatest, forevermore.

I treasure my relationship with Him above all else.

"And indeed, with hardship comes ease." (Quran 94:5)

Imagine finding strength in the promise that every hardship carries the seed of relief. This ayah reminds us to persevere and trust in Allah's plan, knowing that He provides the support we need to navigate life's challenges. May we find solace in our relationship with Allah (SWT), and may His guidance and love be our comfort in times of difficulty.

My Message to You

This poem whispers secrets of the heart, reminding us that even in the shadows of parental absence, forgiveness and healing can bloom. It's a journey of self-discovery, where adversity becomes a stepping stone to understanding and growth. In the tapestry of life, finding solace in Allah's unconditional love is the thread that stitches our stories together. And when challenges arise, perseverance and trust in His plan become the wings that lift us up.

May this poem be a gentle nudge to reflect on your relationships and experiences, and to seek Allah's guidance and support in times of need. May it also remind you that forgiveness, healing, and perseverance are the soft whispers that calm the storms within, guiding you towards a path of peace and purpose. Ameen.

In the tapestry of life, family threads weave a divine pattern of love, laughter, and legacy. A heartfelt ode to cherishing those who bring joy and meaning to our lives, this poem is a gentle reminder to prioritise tenderness, kindness, and compassion, nurturing a haven of peace and love in the sanctuary of home...

"Home is Where the Heart Is, the Best of You"

In the warmth of loved ones' eyes,
I find my peaceful, sacred surprise.
Home is where the heart resides,
Where love and laughter reside, side by side.

The Prophet (PBUH) taught us with care,
"The best of you are those who are best to their families, and I am the best to my family." (Tirmidhi)

What good are we if we don't give
To our families first, and then to others?
If we neglect those closest to our hearts,
What love, what kindness, can we truly impart?

So let us nurture love in our homes,
With tender words, and hearts that roam.
Free from judgment, criticism, and fear,
Embracing each other, year after year.

May Allah (SWT) guide us to prioritise with love,
Our families, our rock, sent from above.
May our homes be filled with laughter, peace, and light,

Reflecting the beauty of our faith, shining so bright.

In the stillness of our hearts, may we find,
The love and care that our families are designed
To receive from us the best of our deeds,
And in return, may our hearts be filled with their love and needs.

"The best of you are those who are best to their families, and I am the best to my family." (Tirmidhi)

Imagine being a gentle breeze on a summer's day, bringing warmth and comfort to those you love. This hadith reminds us that treating our families with kindness, compassion, and love is the greatest reflection of our character. It's a reminder that our homes are sanctuaries where love, laughter, and warmth should flourish.

My Message to You
This poem whispers secrets of the heart, reminding us to tend to our loved ones with kindness, compassion, and love. May it inspire you to create a haven of warmth and light in your home, where laughter and memories are woven into the fabric of everyday life. May your family be a canvas of love, painted with vibrant colours of kindness, empathy, and understanding. May Allah (SWT) guide you to be the best version of yourself for your loved ones, and may

your home be a reflection of the beauty and joy that emanates from your faith. Ameen..

A mother's love is the first whisper of Jannah, a gentle breeze that soothes the soul and nurtures the heart. This heartfelt tribute celebrates the unwavering strength, selfless devotion, and unconditional love of my beloved mother, honouring her legacy and the memories that forever bloom in our hearts...

"A Mother's Love"

A tender touch, a loving gaze,
You guided me through life's maze.
Though struggles came, and hardships too,
Your strength and love saw me through.

As your youngest daughter, I recall,
Helping in the kitchen, learning all.
Cooking, pickling, arts and crafts in hand,
You sold them to support our family, a labour of love to stand.

Your selflessness and dedication shine,
Putting us first, your own needs decline.
I'm grateful for the lessons you taught,
And the memories we shared, a treasure I've sought.

When dementia took hold, and you struggled to recall,
We did our best to care for you, through it all.
Your grandchildren loved the treats you'd make,
A sweet memory they'll forever partake.

Though admitting you to care was hard to do,
We made the decision, with love, to see it through.
Visits and tears, a mix of joy and pain,
Seeing you struggle, weighed heavy on our hearts in vain.

The last visit, holding your hand tight,
Tears streaming down, a moment so bright.
A fleeting glance of recognition, a spark,
Gave me hope, and a memory to mark.

Your passing, a bittersweet refrain,
Sadness and relief, a complex pain.
We miss you dearly and cherish the past,
Grateful for the time we had, and the love that will last.

In Jannah's garden, we'll meet again,
Where love and joy will forever remain.
Until that day, your memory we'll hold,
A mother's love, forever in our hearts, to mould.

"And your Lord has decreed that you worship none but Him. And that you be dutiful to your parents." (Quran 17:23)

Imagine the warmth of a loving home, where kindness, respect, and compassion flow like a gentle stream. This ayah reminds us of the sacred duty we owe to our parents, and the reward for being dutiful to them.

My Message to You
This poem whispers secrets of the heart, reminding us to cherish and honour our parents with love, gratitude, and compassion. May it inspire you to tend to your family relationships with kindness, understanding, and patience, even in the face of challenges and complexities. May you seek Allah's guidance and mercy in times of need, and may your heart be filled with the warmth of love and gratitude. May your relationships be a reflection of the beauty and joy that emanates from your faith, and may you be blessed with peace, love, and harmony. Ameen.

As We Conclude Part 2

As we gently close the pages of **Part 2, "Poems of Love and Connection,"** may the whispers of these words remain in your heart, nurturing love, kindness, and compassion. May the lessons learnt and reflections sparked by these poems guide you towards building strong, resilient bonds with those around you. May we strive to be the best versions of ourselves for our loved ones, just as the Prophet Muhammad (PBUH) taught us, **"The best of you are those who are best to their families."** (Hadith, Narrated by Ibn Majah).

As we embark on new beginnings, may Allah (SWT) bless us with:

- Hearts that overflow with love and kindness
- Minds that shine with understanding and empathy
- Spirits that soar with peace and harmony

May our relationships be a reflection of the beauty and joy that emanates from our faith. May our homes be filled with laughter, peace, and light, and may our bond with one another be strengthened by the threads of love, empathy, and understanding.

As we move forward to **Part 3, "Poems of Hope and Resilience,"** join me on this enchanting journey of exploration and reflection on the human spirit's capacity for hope, resilience, and transformation. May Allah (SWT) guide us towards building strong, loving, and meaningful relationships that bring love, joy, peace, fun, and happiness to our lives.

May our poetic journey be a source of inspiration, guidance, and joy, illuminating our paths towards healing, growth, and transformation. Let's continue to nurture our hearts with hope and resilience, embracing the beauty of relationships that transcend words. May our bond with one another be filled with warmth, compassion, and understanding, and may we emerge from this journey with hearts full of love, kindness, and connection.

Ameen.

PART 3
POEMS OF HOPE AND RESILIENCE
(BEACONS OF LIGHT)

In Beacons of Light, I shine a light on the path forward, offering hope and resilience in the face of challenges, and testifying to the human spirit's capacity for perseverance and growth.

Welcome to **Part 3** of my poetic journey,
"Poems of Hope and Resilience."

As we meander through life's winding paths, where wildflowers of hope and resilience bloom like a whimsical garden, join me on this enchanting journey. Through these poems, may you discover the transformative power of hope and resilience, and may you find guidance, healing, and inspiration in the words that follow. Let's embark on this journey together, where faith, hope, and love converge like a celestial dance, and may our hearts be filled with peace, light, and joy.

Lessons Learnt and Takeaways
As you reflect on the poems in this section, may you take away the following lessons:

1. **River of Trust:**
   Like a river flowing effortlessly to its destination, may we trust in Allah's plan, even when the path ahead seems uncertain. **"And indeed, with hardship comes ease."** (Quran 94:5)

2. **Desert Blooms:**
   Like a garden that blooms in the desert, may hope and resilience flourish in our hearts, even in the most challenging times. **"Do not lose hope, nor be sad."** (Hadith, Narrated by Abu Dawud)

3. **Mercy's Warm Breeze:**
   Like a warm breeze on a summer day, may Allah's mercy envelop us, bringing comfort and guidance in times of need. **"And My mercy encompasses all things."** (Quran 7:156)

4. **Lotus of Self-Discovery:**
   Like a lotus flower unfolding its petals, may we discover the depths of our own hearts, and may self-awareness and introspection guide us towards growth and transformation. **"Know yourself, and you will know Allah."** (Hadith, Narrated by Al-Bukhari)

5. **Compass of Allah's Pleasure:**
   Like a compass pointing towards its true north, may our hearts be guided by the desire to please Allah (SWT), and

may we find peace, happiness, and fulfilment in this pursuit. **"And seek the pleasure of Allah, for indeed, Allah is with those who are patient."** (Quran 8:46)

May our journey be a celestial waltz, filled with hope, resilience, and the light of faith. May our hearts overflow with peace, love, and compassion, and may we emerge from this journey with souls that shine like stars in the velvet night sky, twinkling with joy and wonder. Ameen.

In the intricate fabric of my soul, a story unfolds – a testament to the beauty of self-discovery, the strength of resilience, and the courage of embracing my true essence. Join me on this vibrant journey, where words paint a picture of growth, transformation, and the unwavering pursuit of authenticity. May my story be a gentle breeze that carries the seeds of inspiration, nurturing your own path of self-love, acceptance, and empowerment. May you bloom into the most radiant version of yourself, unapologetically unique and beautifully alive...

"A Mixed Heritage, A Unique Soul"

In childhood's haze, I wandered alone,
A mixed heritage, a heart of stone.
I searched for belonging, a place to call home,
But judgemental eyes made my heart feel unknown.

In school, I found solace in sports and might,
A sense of pride and accomplishment, shining bright.
I excelled in athletics, and for a moment, I was free,
From the chains of judgement, from the weight of being me.

Academically, I was average, but I didn't give up the fight,
I learnt to navigate, to find my own light.
In a world that didn't understand me, I found my way,
Through darkness and pain, I emerged, stronger each day.

High school was a journey, a test of will and might,
But it taught me valuable lessons, guiding me through the night.
Of self-acceptance, resilience, and pride,
Embracing my uniqueness, letting my spirit glide.

In the corporate world, I faced new challenges and strived to be my best,

Working under apartheid, with its awful unrest.
I tried to fit in, to conform to the culture within,
But the more I tried, the more I realised it wasn't who I was
meant to be, and I decided to embrace my authentic self at last.

I faced staring eyes, envy, and sometimes unrest,
But I stayed true to myself, made many unhappy, yet my integrity
was intact.
There were those who taught me not to give up and fight for
what I believed in, no matter the plight.
I thank them for seeing me, for reminding me of my worth.

Today, here I am, loving me for me,
Allah's guidance rescued me, set my soul free.
As the Quran says, "And indeed, with hardship comes ease."
(Quran 94:5)

So if you're lost and alone, searching for a place to belong,
Just know you're not alone, and your story is not wrong.
Embrace your heritage, culture, and soul,
And know that you are strong, your spirit will make you whole.

"Every person is born with a natural disposition (Fitrah); it is his parents who make him a Jew or a Christian or a Magian." (Sahih Bukhari)

A reminder that our innate nature is pure, and it's the world around us that shapes our identities.

My Message to You
Like a delicate petal unfolding, may you bloom into your true self. May the gentle rain of self-acceptance and the warm sunshine of resilience nourish your soul. Shine bright like a star, and may your life be a celestial dance of kindness, love, and light. Ameen...

When delays unfold into blessings, our hearts are stirred, and our souls are reminded of Allah's loving plan. In its gentle wisdom, we find solace, guidance, and a call to trust in the heart's deepest longing...

"When Delays are Blessings"

In Allah's divine plan, delays unfold
To test our faith, to refine and mould
Our hearts to His will, our souls to His way
To strengthen our trust, day by day.

The Prophet's words echo through time
"Perhaps Allah delays, to bring something sublime"
So let us trust, and not lose our stride
For in delays, Allah's wisdom abides.

He knows what's best in every test
And His delays are blessings, we must attest
In the Quran, Allah's words shine bright
"And perhaps you dislike, what's good for your sight."

So let us surrender, and trust in His plan
And see delays as blessings, in His loving hand
For He is the All-Knowing, the All-Wise
And His delays are opportunities, to rise and thrive.

When worries creep, and delays seem long
Remember Allah's mercy, and His loving song

He guides us through every single test
And weaves delays into blessings, we'll love best.
In His gentle hands, our dreams take flight
Like a rose in bloom, our hearts shine bright
The wait may seem long, but trust in His decree
For Allah's delays are gifts of love, sent specially.

So breathe, dear heart, and let your soul revive
In the stillness, hear Allah's whisper, "You are alive"
He's writing our story, with every single line
And delays are just commas that make His blessings shine.

In the Quran, Allah's promise is clear
"My mercy encompasses all things, dear"
So hold on to hope, and never lose your way
For Allah's delays are blessings coming your way.

"And perhaps you dislike something, but it is good for you."
(Quran 4:19)

Imagine delays as a gentle whisper, guiding you toward Allah's plan and presence. This ayah reminds us that sometimes what seems unfavourable can lead to growth, guidance, and blessings.

My Message to You

May the words of this poem be a gentle breeze that carries the whispers of hope and guidance, leading you closer to Allah's loving heart. May its message inspire a deeper sense of trust and connection, and may you find comfort, peace, and joy in the beauty of Allah's plan. May Allah's love and guidance be your constant companion, illuminating your path and filling your heart with joy and devotion. Ameen.

When darkness fades, and Allah's light prevails, our hearts are stirred, and our souls are reminded of His loving presence. In its gentle radiance, we find solace, guidance, and a call to trust in the heart's deepest longing...

"When Darkness Fades, Allah's Light Prevails"

In life's most desperate hour, when death's shadow loomed near,
And Shaytan's grip seemed strong, our hearts trembled with fear.
But Allah (SWT), our Merciful Saviour, heard our silent plea,
And with His loving kindness, set our souls free.

He lifted us from the abyss and guided us to His light,
A beacon of hope in darkness that shone with pure delight.
Our hearts, once shattered and lost, He mended with care,
And in His forgiveness, our spirits were lifted, beyond compare.

With every breath, we thank Him for His mercy and might,
For saving us from the edge and leading us to His loving light.
In His presence, we find peace, our souls forever at rest,
A sense of belonging to His divine love, forever at its best.

Oh, Allah (SWT), our Beloved, Your love we cannot contain,
Your mercy, we cannot fathom, Your guidance, we cannot explain.
You are the Owner of our hearts, the Sovereign of our souls,
Forever we'll worship You, with hearts that beat with love's goals.

Now and forever, we strive, Your servants, humble and true,
To gain a place in Jannah's gardens, where love and joy shine through.
We yearn to hear Your words, "Enter, My servants, into My mercy and bliss,"
And dwell in Your presence, forever, in eternal peace and happiness.

May our lives be a testament to Your transformative power,
A shining example of Your love, in every hour.
May we forever walk in the warmth of Your loving light,
And may our hearts remain forever grateful, day and night.

May it warm your heart, inspire your soul, and remind you of Allah's infinite love and mercy.
May we forever cherish the gift of faith,
and may our hearts remain filled with love, devotion,
and praise for Allah (SWT), the Almighty.

And remember, dear friend, that whenever darkness falls,
And challenges seem insurmountable, never give up!
Reach out for help, call upon Allah (SWT), and seek guidance from those who care.

For in the words of the Quran,
"So verily, with every difficulty, there is relief" (94:5).
May Allah's peace, comfort, and strength be with you always.
Ameen.

"Allah is nearer to His servant than the jugular vein." (Hadith)

Imagine Allah's presence as a gentle whisper, guiding you through life's challenges and triumphs. This hadith reminds us that Allah is always near, watching over us with love and care.

My Message to You
May the words of this poem be a beacon of hope, guiding you towards Allah's love and mercy. May its message inspire deeper gratitude, trust, and connection, and may you find comfort, peace, and joy in the wisdom of Allah's plan. May Allah's love and guidance be your constant companion, now and always. Ameen.

As I dance with the shadows, I've learnt to dive deep within, to let go of the weight that binds, and to unfurl like a blooming flower. Healing has taught me to be gentle with myself, to whisper sweet nothings to my soul, and to trust in Allah (SWT). Alhumdulilah, I am grateful for this journey, for the lessons learnt, and for the growth that has unfolded like a masterpiece...

"A Journey of Healing"

Healing has whispered secrets to my soul,
To dive deep within and let go of the role.
Not to take things personally, a lesson so fine,
And to be gentle with myself, in this journey divine.

I'm grateful for this space of calmness I've found,
Indescribable growth, a heart that's turned around.
I thank Allah (SWT) for guiding me on this path,
Alhumdulilah, I'm trusting in His loving wrath.

As I break free from generational chains,
I hope to change not just my life, but also the lives of those I sustain.
My loved ones, friends, and all those I meet,
May my journey inspire, and our hearts skip a beat.

By sharing my story, I hope to make a difference true,
In at least one person's life, a change, a renewal anew.
Gratitude to Allah (SWT), for this journey I embark on,
May His love and guidance forever shine in my heart.

"And We will surely test you with something of fear and hunger and a loss of wealth and lives and fruits but give good tidings to the patient." (Quran 2:155)

Imagine life's challenges as a canvas, painted with vibrant colours of growth and transformation. This ayah reminds us that trials are opportunities for patience, perseverance, and spiritual growth.

My Message to You

May my story be a reminder that healing is possible, that growth is attainable, and that Allah's love is always available. May you find peace, comfort, and inspiration in these words, and may you be encouraged to embark on your own journey of healing and self-discovery. Ameen.

Imagine life's journey as a majestic canvas, painted with vibrant colours of wonder, curiosity, and adventure. As we navigate the twists and turns, may our hearts be filled with faith, hope, and trust in Allah's loving guidance. May every step be a testament to His mercy and care, and may our souls be nourished by the beauty of His presence...

"Journeying Through Life Guided by Faith"

With every step I take, I know I'm not alone,
Guided by faith, through life's unknown.
The path may wind, and the journey may seem long,
But Allah's promise echoes, "With hardship comes ease, and you will be strong" (Quran 94:5)

In times of struggle, when doubts creep in,
I hold on to hope and the promise within.
That Allah (SWT) is with me, guiding every step,
And though the road ahead may seem uncertain, I'll keep

Moving forward, through life's joys and fears,
I know that Allah's plan is filled with tears of happiness and laughter through the years.
The best is yet to come, Insha'Allah, I believe,
And with each breath, my faith and trust in Allah's mercy, I receive.

So I'll persevere through every test,
Knowing Allah's support is always at its best.
And when the journey ends, and my time on earth is done,

I pray that Allah (SWT) welcomes me with a heart that's pure,
and a soul that's won.

Ameen., Ya Rabb, may this be my fate,
Guided by faith, and blessed with Your mercy, great.

"Allah is Beautiful and loves beauty." (Sahih Muslim)

Imagine Allah's beauty as a radiant sunrise, painting the sky with vibrant colours of love, mercy, and kindness. This hadith reminds us that beauty is not just a reflection of the physical world, but also a manifestation of Allah's attributes.

My Message to You
May your heart dance with hope and trust, knowing that Allah's guidance and mercy are like a warm breeze on a summer day, always available to soothe your soul. May hardships become the fertile soil where seeds of growth and ease take root, and may faith and trust be the wings that lift you to new heights. May perseverance and hope be the gentle rains that nourish your spirit, leading you to a brighter, more radiant future.

May this poem be a gentle reminder that Allah's love and mercy are woven into the fabric of your life, and may you trust in His plan with every fibre of your being. Ameen.

In the gentle whispers of faith, may the strength and beauty of Muslim women be celebrated. This poem is a tender tribute to the radiant souls who weave together the threads of family, community, and spirituality with love, resilience, and dignity...

"Women of Islam"

Oh, women of Islam, know your worth and divine gift,
The strength to bear children and nurture with love and lift.
The roles you play, a mother, sister, aunt, grandmother, friend, and wife.
May you fill each one with purpose and thrive in Allah's divine life.

You are the backbone of society, the nurturer of the earth,
Your role in motherhood, a blessing of immense worth.
The Quran says, "And We have enjoined upon man to be good to his parents;
his mother bore him in weakness upon weakness" (31:14).

Your education and knowledge, a fundamental right,
As encouraged by the Prophet, who said, "Seeking knowledge is an obligation upon every Muslim."
Your financial independence, a freedom to pursue,
As stated in Surah An-Nisa, "And do not give your property, which Allah has made for you a means of support, to the foolish" (4:5).

You are the guardians of your families, the keepers of the faith,
Your modesty and humility, a shield against life's temptations and weight.

Follow the teachings of the Quran and the example of the Prophet's wives,
Who were strong, intelligent, and courageous in their faith and their lives.
Be the Muslim woman you were meant to be, a woman of strength, resilience, and dignity.

May Allah (SWT) guide you, and grant you wisdom, and grace. And may you always remember your worth and your sacred place.

Ameen.

"And indeed, the men who submit to Allah and the women who submit to Allah, and the believing men and believing women, and the obedient men and obedient women, and the truthful men and truthful women, and the patient men and patient women, and the humble men and humble women, and the charitable men and charitable women, and the fasting men and fasting women, and the men who guard their private parts and the women who do so, and the men who remember Allah often and the women who do so - for them Allah has prepared forgiveness and a great reward." (Quran 33:35)

Like a sprinkle of morning magic that whispers secrets of faith, reminding us of the sparkles of submission, obedience, truthfulness, patience, humility, charity, and modesty.

My Message to You
May this poem be a sweet serenade that harmonises with your soul, inspiring you to bloom into a masterpiece of faith, self-love, and confidence. May its gentle rhythm guide you towards a deeper dance with Allah's love and guidance, and may you twirl in the joy and peace of His divine presence. Ameen..

When kindness whispers sweet nothings to our soul, we discover that life's symphony is composed of empathy, love, compassion, and gentle kindness. It's a masterpiece of serving others, where every note resonates with purpose.

This poem is a love letter to the art of living with intention, where every brushstroke paints a picture of love, kindness, and compassion. May its words inspire you to create a masterpiece of purpose, leaving a trail of warmth and light for others to follow.

May your essence shine bright, illuminating the path for others, and may your heart overflow with the joy of serving, loving, and kindness. Make your essence count, and let love be the legacy you leave behind...

"Living with Purpose"

Living with purpose, a life of design,
Not just seeking happiness but serving with a divine mind.
Empathy, love, compassion, and kindness we impart,
The greatest gift we give, a treasure to the heart.

In acts of kindness, we find our way,
Pleasing our Creator, each and every day.
This life is not just about our own delight,
But shining a light in the darkest of nights.

We choose our essence, our purpose in this life,
To make a difference, to cut through strife.
To leave a legacy of love and kindness true,
A purpose-driven life, with a heart that's anew.

So let's make our essence count, each and every day,
With every breath, with every step, with every way.
Let's spread love, kindness, and compassion far and wide,
Living our purpose, with a heart full of pride.

May Allah (SWT) guide us on this journey we embark on,
And may our lives be a reflection of our purpose in the dark.

Ameen.

> "And indeed, you are on an exalted standard of character."
> (Quran 68:4)

May this ayah be the gentle morning dew that nourishes the garden of your soul, cultivating the blooms of moral excellence, guiding you towards a life of purpose, compassion, and radiant character, like a sunrise that paints the sky with vibrant hues of hope and promise.

My Message to You

May this poem be the gentle breeze that carries the seeds of kindness, compassion, and love, nurturing a garden of purpose in your heart. May your life bloom with the beauty of moral excellence, and may your legacy be a symphony of love and kindness that touches hearts and inspires souls. Ameen.

As we ponder the words "Survive Alone," let's gently ask ourselves: Is this the path that brings us peace? Or does it lead to loneliness and chaos? Let's take a deep breath and explore the freedom of taking back control of our nafs /ego, unlearning unhealthy patterns, and mastering healthier habits.

May this poem guide you towards the serenity of self-awareness, the empowerment of self-control, and the joy of nurturing healthier relationships with yourself, others, and your Creator. May you find peace, happiness, and transformation on this journey of self-discovery...

"Taking Back Control (Nafs/Ego)"

In the silence, I reflect on words so true,
"Survive Alone," a path that's lonely, too.
Is this really what I seek? Is this my heart's desire?
Or will it lead me down a road of chaos and a soul on fire?

I've walked that path and felt the pain,
Of loneliness, and a heart in vain.
But then I learnt to take back control,
Of my nafs/ego, and let my spirit unfold.

It's a journey of self-discovery, of growth, and of might,
Unlearning unhealthy habits and shining with new light.
Mastering the What? When? Why? Who? and How?,
To break free from chains that bound me somehow.

With every step, I feel my heart revive,
My relationships transform, and my soul starts to thrive.
The fruits of my labour, a harvest so divine,
Peace, happiness, and love, that's truly mine.

Ya Rabb, guide me on this path, I pray,
Help me take back control, day by day.

May I be aware of the role I play,
In my relationships and every step of the way.

May I continue to transform and grow,
With Your guidance and protection, my Beloved Rabb, I know.
May I do right, by myself, and others, too,
And may my heart be filled with love and all that's true.

Ameen.

"Indeed, Allah will not change the condition of a people until they change what is in themselves." (Quran 13:11)

May this ayah be the soft breeze that stirs the wings of your soul, awakening the gentle art of transformation, guiding you toward growth like a blooming flower, peace like a serene lake, and happiness like a warm ray of sunshine.

My Message to You

May this poem be the spark that ignites your journey of self-discovery and growth, inspiring you to take control of your thoughts, emotions, and actions. May you find guidance, support, and peace in Allah's loving presence, and may your life be transformed by the power of internal change. Ameen.

In the midst of turmoil, we seek Your gentle touch, O Allah (SWT). May Your love and guidance be the calm in every storm, and may Your protection be the shelter from life's tempests...

"Dedication to all Believers"

Dedicated to all believers facing catastrophes around the world,
May Allah's loving arms envelop you, like a warm, gentle curl.
May His guidance, love, blessings, and protection be your shield,
Comforting your hearts, easing your pain, and healing your wounds so real.

May Allah's mercy and compassion be your solace and strength,
May His love and care dispel your fears and guide you to a brighter length. May He grant you patience and perseverance in your trials.
And may He lead you to peace, and an eternal smile that never grows old.

And know that your sacrifice is not in vain,
For Jannah awaits you, with its gates open wide in gain,
A paradise of bliss, where love and joy reside,
Where Allah's pleasure is the greatest prize inside.

May your hearts be filled with hope and peace.
May your souls be comforted with the promise of release,
From the trials of this world to the bliss of the hereafter,
May Allah (SWT) guide you, and to the path that's laughter.
Ameen.

> "And indeed, with hardship comes ease." (Quran 94:5)

May this divine promise be the soft breeze that carries the seeds of hope and comfort to your soul. May every challenge be a stepping stone to relief and peace, and may Allah's love and guidance illuminate your path.

My Message to You

May this poem be a whisper of hope and comfort, reminding you that You are never alone in Your struggles. May Allah's mercy and compassion envelop You, and may His peace be the balm that soothes Your soul. May You find strength in His presence and emerge from every challenge more radiant and resilient. Ameen.

Sow Seeds of Righteousness, and may this poem be the gentle rain that nourishes your soul, reminding you to prioritise Allah's pleasure and build a strong foundation for your Akhirah. May you bloom with sincerity, flourish with devotion, and harvest the fruits of Jannah. Let go of societal whispers and tune into the sweet melody of your Creator's guidance...

"Society's Expectations vs. Allah's Pleasure"

Oh, society, why do we succumb to your pressure?
Why do we strive to live up to others' expectations, like a never-ending measure?
When our focus should be on pleasing our One True Rabb,
And living up to His expectations, for that's all that truly matters, and will forever last.

We're running a rat race, chasing things that fade,
While neglecting our Akhirah, and the life that's yet to be made.
This life is but a test, a trial of our character and will,
So let's redirect our focus and build our foundation still.

Let's lay the bricks of righteousness, one by one,
And build a strong foundation, for our Akhirah has just begun.
Let's focus on pleasing Allah (SWT) and earning our place in Jannah's shade,
For that's the ultimate reward and the greatest prize we can ever trade.

Our Rabb hears and knows all, and sees the depths of our heart,
So let's be true to ourselves and never depart
From the path of righteousness, and the way of the true,

For Jannah awaits those who are sincere, and their hearts are anew.

Now's the time to choose, to restart, and to begin,
To be the best version of ourselves and let our spirits win.
Our Rabb awaits us with open arms and a heart full of love,
So let's choose wisely and rise above.

"And indeed, this is My straight path, so follow it, and do not follow [other] paths, for they will separate you from His way."
(Quran 6:153)

May this divine guidance be the gentle breeze that whispers direction to your soul, keeping you on the path of righteousness and illuminating your journey with Allah's love.

My Message to You
May your heart bloom with devotion, and your soul shine with sincerity. May Allah's pleasure be the rhythm that harmonises your life, and Jannah be the garden you're nurturing with every step. May you find freedom in faith, strength in values, and peace in pleasing your Lord. May your Akhirah be your masterpiece, crafted with love, and your spirit soar on the wings of devotion. Ameen.

As We Conclude Part 3

As we gently close the pages of **Part 3, "Poems of Hope and Resilience,"** may the whispers of these words remain in your heart, nurturing hope, resilience, and faith. May the lessons learnt and reflections sparked by these poems guide you towards a brighter, more compassionate future.

May we strive to be like a garden that blooms in the desert, where hope and resilience flourish in the harshest of conditions. May our hearts overflow with hope and resilience, just as the Quran reminds us, **"And indeed, with hardship comes ease."** (Quran 94:5)

As we embark on new beginnings, may Allah (SWT) bless us with:

- Hearts that overflow with hope and resilience
- Minds that shine with wisdom and understanding

- Spirits that soar with peace and positivity

May our lives be a reflection of the beauty and joy that emanates from our faith. May our bond with one another be strengthened by the threads of empathy, compassion, and understanding.

As we move forward to **Part 4, "Poems of Reflection and Growth,"** join me on this enchanting journey of self-discovery and spiritual development. May Allah (SWT) guide us towards building a deeper connection with ourselves, others, and our faith. May our poetic journey be a source of inspiration, guidance, and joy, illuminating our paths towards healing, growth, and transformation.

May our hearts be filled with love, kindness, and connection, and may we emerge from this journey with souls that shine like stars in the night sky.

Ameen.

PART 4

POEMS OF REFLECTION AND GROWTH
(JOURNEY WITHIN)

In Journey Within, I invite you to reflect on personal growth, self-awareness, and the journey of life, exploring the human experience with all its triumphs and struggles.

Welcome to **Part 4** of my poetic journey,
"Poems of Reflection and Growth."

As reflection's gentle light touches our souls, the heart yearns for growth, wisdom, and peace. Join me on this poetic journey, where words become whispers of insight, and verses bloom into flowers of hope. May these poems be the soft breeze that soothes your heart, inspiring you to cultivate resilience, nurture hope, and seek guidance. May they ignite a spark of self-awareness, compassion, and understanding that illuminates your path and guides you towards a brighter, wiser you. Let's wander this winding path together, where reflection and growth converge, and may our hearts be filled with the peace of self-discovery, the joy of learning, and the beauty of a soul that flourishes.

Lessons Learnt and Takeaways

As you wander through these poems, may gentle wisdom unfold, like petals of a flower sharing their secrets. May the following lessons be the soft breeze that whispers guidance to your heart:

1. **Appreciate Allah's Creation:**
   May nature's beauty bloom gratitude and awe in your heart, like a garden that flourishes with every sunrise. **"Indeed, in the creation of the heavens and the earth, there are signs for a people who reflect."** (Quran 3:190)

2. **Honour Resilience:**
   May the stories of others' journeys ignite kindness and compassion in your soul, like a gentle breeze that soothes and heals. **"The believers are like a single body. If one part of it is injured, the whole body feels the pain."** (Hadith, Narrated by Muslim)

3. **Nurture Self-Love:**
   May self-care and healthy boundaries be the soft whispers that nurture your well-being, like a calm lake that reflects the beauty of the sky. **"Do not obey the orders of the extravagant. Indeed, He does not like those who commit excess."** (Quran 7:31)

4. **Cultivate Kindness:** May compassion and empathy be the fragrance that fills your heart and touches others' lives, like a rose that blooms in every season. **"None of you truly**

believes, until he loves for his brother, what he loves for himself." (Bukhari)

May our journey be a dance of reflection, growth, and love. May our hearts overflow with peace, and may our souls shine like stars in the night sky, illuminating the path for ourselves and others. Ameen.

As the day's final light dances across the horizon, may our souls be drawn to the beauty of the divine. May the whispers of dua guide us on our journey, and may the glow of sunset ignite a fire of devotion in our hearts. In the pursuit of spiritual growth, may we find peace, guidance, and rebirth...

"Chasing Sunsets to the Ends of the Earth"

Chasing sunsets to the ends of the earth,
A journey of devotion, a path of spiritual rebirth.
With every step, a new horizon unfolds,
A tapestry of Allah's beauty, a story yet untold.

Through mountains and valleys, I wander and roam,
Following the sunset's glow, to the edges of my spiritual home.
With each new dusk, my heart beats anew,
A sense of gratitude, a spirit that's true.

The call to prayer whispers secrets of Allah's majesty and might,
and I am drawn to the mystery, like a believer in the night.
My soul takes flight on the wings of prayer and devotion,
And I am one with Allah (SWT), my journey to Jannah in motion.

So I'll keep chasing sunsets, to the ends of the earth,
For in their glow, I find my heart, my soul, my spiritual rebirth.
And when the journey ends, and the sun dips in the west,
I'll carry Allah's radiance forever in my chest.

> "Indeed, in the creation of the heavens and the earth, and the alternation of the night and the day, there are signs for a people who reflect." (Quran 3:190 or 10:6, similar ayah)

May the whispers of nature's beauty be the gentle lullaby that rocks your soul into the majesty of Allah's presence, and may your heart overflow with gratitude like a blooming garden, wonder like a twinkling starry night, and awe like a majestic mountain peak.

My Message to You

May this poem be the soft whisper of the wind that awakens your soul to the magic of spiritual growth, guiding you to discover the hidden treasures of creation. May you find solace in devotion like a flower finding nourishment in the sun, peace in dua like a gentle stream flowing to its destination, and rebirth in the radiance of Allah (SWT) like a butterfly emerging from its cocoon.

May your spirit soar on the wings of reflection like a bird riding the thermals of dawn, and may your heart overflow with the joy of connection like a garden blooming with love, and the peace of spiritual growth like a serene moonlit night. Ameen.

In the tapestry of trials, Gaza's story is woven with threads of resilience, faith, and courage. May this poem be a gentle breeze that carries the whispers of solidarity, empathy, and admiration for those who have suffered, yet remain steadfast in their devotion. May it inspire others to draw strength from their unwavering commitment to their faith, and may their sacrifices be a beacon of hope, illuminating the path to spiritual growth and the promise of Jannah..."

"Tribute to the Chosen Ones"

In October's darkness, a tale unfolded in pain,
In Palestine's streets, horror and grief did reign.
Yet, amidst the tragedy, a beacon shone so bright,
The chosen ones stood firm in faith's unwavering light.

Their paths, decreed by Allah (SWT), the King of Kings above,
Showed us that He precedes all, in endless, boundless love.
Every life lost, every sacrifice made, every dua whispered low,
Reminded us of His majesty, His omnipotence, as the tears did flow.

As I reflect on their journey, my heart is filled with sorrow and warmth,
A mix of emotions, as I realise our worldly comforts are but a fragile form.
We, who remain in comfort's bubble, surrounded by possessions galore,
Are, in truth, at a loss, for we've forgotten what truly matters, and what we adore.

For you, dear chosen ones, Jannah's gates are Open wide,
Filled with bliss, eternal peace, where love and joy reside.

Your faith, courage, and devotion to Deen have inspired us all,
A shining example that guides us through life's turbulent squall.

May Allah's guidance and protection reside within your hearts,
As you walk the path that's been decreed from the very start.
I strive to follow in your footsteps to prove my worthiness true,
To earn Allah's pleasure, and meet you, in Jannah's gardens, anew.

Until that day, when bliss resides, and love shines bright and bold,
I am honoured to walk in your footsteps on the path that's been decreed, to unfold.
May Allah (SWT) bless you, grant you peace, and reunite us, in Jannah's shade,
Where love, joy, and tranquillity forever will be displayed.

"And do not think of those who have been killed in the cause of Allah as dead. Rather, they are alive with their Lord, receiving provision." (Quran 3:169)

This ayah whispers sweet nothings of eternal life, reminding us that those who have sacrificed for the sake of Allah (SWT) are dancing in the gardens of paradise, their souls nourished by divine ambrosia, and their hearts overflowing with joy.

My Message to You

May this poem be a soft breeze that carries the fragrance of their legacy, inspiring you to honour their memories with love, gratitude, and devotion. May their stories ignite a spark of spiritual growth within you, and may you trust in the promise of eternal life like a child trusts in the warmth of a loving embrace. May Allah (SWT) bless you with courage that soars like an eagle, devotion that blooms like a rose, and peace that flows like a gentle stream. Ameen.

As gentle wisdom whispers secrets to the heart, may our souls tend to the garden within, nurturing self-love, self-respect, and self-care. May boundaries be the soft breeze that soothes the soul, reminding us of our worth and guiding us to prioritise our own needs. In the dance of life, may our spirits soar with freedom, and may our hearts overflow with peace, kindness, and justice, like a garden in full bloom...

"Establishing Healthy Boundaries"

With self-love, self-respect, and self-care in mind,
I set boundaries to protect my heart and soul, entwined.
As Allah (SWT) guides, "Do not obey the orders of the extravagant." (Quran 7:31)
I prioritise my needs and recognise my own worth, magnificent.

I'm not being selfish, but wise, I've come to see,
That I must fill my own cup before pouring out to others, generously.
For Allah (SWT) reminds me, "I do not burden a soul beyond that it can bear..." (Quran 2:286)
So I take care of myself and set boundaries with love and care.

I acknowledge my limits and learn to say "no",
Not to restrict, but to preserve my energy and make it grow.
I prioritise my well-being and nurture my soul,
Remembering Allah's words, "Indeed, Allah orders justice and good conduct." (Quran 16:90)

May I find strength, courage, and wisdom every day,
To establish healthy boundaries and prioritise my own way.

May I remember, I'm worthy of love, care, and respect,
From myself and others, and may Allah's peace be my perfect protector.

"Do not obey the orders of the extravagant." (Quran 7:31) or more accurately **"And do not be extravagant. Indeed, He does not like those who commit excess."**

This ayah whispers sweet nothings of balance and harmony, reminding us to waltz through life with gentle steps, avoiding the discordant notes of excessiveness and extravagance, and instead embracing the melody of moderation and self-awareness.

My Message to You
May this poem be the gentle morning dew that nourishes your soul's garden, inspiring you to tend to your inner blooms of self-love, self-respect, and self-care. May it guide you to prune the weeds of negativity, water the seeds of wisdom, and harvest the fruits of courage and self-awareness. May your heart overflow with peace like a serene lake, kindness like a warm breeze, and compassion like a gentle rain. Ameen.

As the whispers of kindness caress the soul, may our words be balm, and our actions be love. May this poem guide us to tend to the hearts of others with compassion and empathy, and may we seek wisdom in the gentle guidance of Allah's love...

"You Can't Fix Yourself by Hurting Others"

In the gentle breeze of Allah's love,
We find solace, sent from above.
The Quran's words, a guiding light,
Remind us that kindness is what makes our hearts take flight.

"That no soul shall bear another's burden." (Quran 35:18)
A promise that our healing can't be built on pain.
The Prophet's (PBUH) wisdom echoes in our hearts,
"None of you truly believes, until he loves for his brother, what he loves for himself." (Bukhari)

Let's wrap each other in love and compassion's fold,
And find our healing, in the warmth of hearts made of gold.
In every smile, a blessing is shared,
In every kindness, a heart is repaired.

May our actions be a reflection of Allah's grace,
And may our love for each other fill every space.
For in the beauty of kindness, we find our peaceful nest,
And the love we share with others becomes the healing balm we've been blessed with.

"That no soul shall bear another's burden." (Quran 35:18)

This ayah whispers gentle reminders that our choices are like ripples on a pond, and we are the masters of our own destiny.

"None of you truly believes, until he loves for his brother, what he loves for himself." (Bukhari)

This teaching whispers sweet nothings of empathy and kindness, guiding us to treat others with the same tender love and respect we'd cherish for ourselves.

My Message to You
May this poem be the soft petals of a rose that gently touch your heart, inspiring kindness, compassion, and empathy to bloom. May it nurture a garden of love and understanding, where words are balm for the soul, and actions reflect the divine love that guides you. Ameen.

May the gentle whispers of life's journey guide us to cherish each moment as a precious gift, and may the beauty of growth, learning, and self-discovery unfold within us. May this poem inspire us to walk the path of courage, hope, and determination, trusting in the divine plan and guidance that unfolds with every step...

"Life's Journey of Growth"

In life's tapestry, experiences weave,
Journey of growth, learning, and self-discovery to achieve.
Every moment, a lesson to share,
Joyful or challenging, each one helps us care.

Through loving, listening, and learning from our mistakes,
We gather life's pieces, transforming heartaches.
Into wisdom, like a phoenix rising high,
From ashes of struggles, we touch the sky.

Allah's (SWT) words echo, a guiding light,
"And indeed, with hardship comes ease." (Quran 94:5)
A promise that every storm will pass,
And relief will follow, like a gentle summer breeze at last.

And when the darkness falls, and fears arise,
I hold on to Allah's promise, "And We will surely test you with something of fear." (Quran 2:155)
But I know that after fear comes peace, and Allah's mercy shines,
A reminder that He is always near, a constant, loving guide.

So let us persevere, through life's highs and lows,
Learning from each experience, as our wisdom grows.
Trusting Allah's plan, with hearts full of cheer,

We'll overcome obstacles and emerge stronger, year by year.

May Allah (SWT) guide us, through life's journey so grand,
And fill our lives with wisdom, love, and peace, in this world and the next,

Ameen.

"And indeed, with hardship comes ease." (Quran 94:5)

This ayah whispers sweet nothings of hope and reassurance, reminding us that challenges are like fleeting clouds, and relief is forthcoming like a warm sunrise.

My Message to You
May this poem be the soft whispers of the wind that stirs your soul, guiding you to transform life's journey into a masterpiece of growth, wisdom, and love, like a painter adding brushstrokes of beauty to a canvas. May Allah's promise of ease after hardship be your North Star, shining bright with hope, and may your heart overflow with peace like a serene lake, love like a blooming garden, and trust like a gentle stream. Ameen.

May our children bloom like gardens, nurtured by love and guided by faith. May we recognise them as blessings, not possessions, and trust in Allah's plan as we guide them. May our hearts be filled with humility, and our hands be gentle, as we walk the path of parenting with love, trust, and surrender...

"Our Children Are Blessings, Not Possessions"

Our children are blessings, not possessions; we must understand,
A truth that echoes, loud and clear, across this land.
Our Rabb is the Creator, the Owner of all we see,
Who are we to disrespect what He's given us, in His decree?

Wake up, dear parent, wake up, and take heed,
Own your mistakes, listen, learn, grow, and heal, indeed.
Listen to your children; don't just hear their words,
For there's a difference, come what may, in these two verbs.

Take time to understand them, to improve your bond,
Treat them as rare gifts, polished, but not beyond.
Life is a journey; let them grow from their choices.
Lessons will be learnt, and patience will be the voice.

Enforcing your way leads to pain,
Stifling their growth and causing them to stray.
Drugs, bad company, parental abuse, and more,
Become a norm, something we all abhor.

Shaytan loves and strives on pain,
And choices that lead us away from Deen and our Rabb's reign.

He whispers deceit and fuels our pride,
Leading us astray, and deep inside.

But we must resist and stand strong,
Guiding our children and keeping them from wrong.
Give them space to breathe, to learn as they go,
Making their own choices and growing from their "no's".

Trust in Allah's plan for them, and do your best,
Guide them to the straight path and leave the rest.
Trust is what it takes to let go and be free,
To know that Allah (SWT) knows best, and that's all we need to see.

So, do your best, and leave it all in Allah's hands,
For He knows what's best, and His plan is grand.

"And know that your properties and your children are but a trial and that Allah has with Him a great reward." (Quran 8:28)

May this ayah whisper sweet nothings of trust and responsibility, reminding us that our little blessings are precious gifts, and our role as guardians is a sacred trust.

My Message to You
May this poem be the gentle caress of a summer breeze that stirs your heart, guiding you to cherish your precious gifts with love that nurtures, humility that learns, and trust that soars. May your journey of parenting be a dance of joy, filled with whispers of wisdom, and may your soul overflow with peace like a gentle fountain, knowing that Allah's guidance is always near, like a loving parent's embrace. Ameen.

May tender threads of love weave our family ties, whispering kindness, understanding, and forgiveness into the hearts of our precious children. In the garden of Jannah, may our bond bloom forever, nurtured by devotion, compassion, and the beauty of imperfection...

"Be Good to Your Parents"

Oh, children, oh children of mankind.
Be kind to your parents, for all time.
Forgive us for not being what you want.
Know, we were created just for you, a precious gift from Allah (SWT), supreme and true.

We may not be perfect, and that's okay,
Let's accept that we come uniquely wrapped each day.
Forgive our shortcomings, and all that we do,
That may not please you, but know that we're trying our best, for me and for you.

We'll make mistakes along the way,
But please understand, we're trying every day.
To be patient, kind, and loving, too,
And to understand you, as you grow and learn anew.

Take time to listen and understand our plight,
We're doing our best, with all our might.
Know that we can't do this alone,
But with your love and support, we'll find our way back home.

Let's work together to earn our place,
At the gates of Jannah, where love and peace entwine in a warm embrace.
May Allah (SWT) guide us on this journey we share,
And fill our hearts with love, and show us we care.

We love you forevermore,
And promise to be there, through every joy and every roar.
So be kind to your parents, and remember our plea,
We're trying our best to be the best family.

"And We have enjoined upon man [to be good to his parents. His mother carried him, increasing her] in weakness upon weakness, and his weaning is in two years. Be grateful to Me and to your parents; to Me is the [final destination." (Quran 31:14)

May this ayah whisper sweet nothings of gratitude and love, reminding us of the selfless devotion of our parents, like a gentle stream that nourishes our souls. May it guide us to treat them with kindness that soothes, respect that uplifts, and compassion that heals, as we journey towards our ultimate destination, where love and devotion are the currency of the heart, and pleasing Allah (SWT) is the greatest treasure.

My Message to You

May this poem be a gentle breeze that stirs your heart, inspiring you to cherish your parents with love, kindness, and gratitude. May it guide you to build strong, loving relationships with your family, and may your heart overflow with compassion and appreciation for the sacrifices of those who have nurtured you. May Allah (SWT) guide us to be good to our parents, and may He reward us with love, kindness, and a place in Jannah, Ameen.

May tender threads of kindness weave our words and deeds, as we journey through life's precious moments. May our interactions be infused with love, compassion, and peace, reflecting the beauty of our faith...

"Valuing the Efforts of Others"

In the beauty of connection, we find our way,
To nurture bonds and seize each new day.
A simple response, truthful and kind,
Can bridge the gaps and soothe the mind.

It costs nothing, yet means everything,
To reply with love and a heart that sings.
A gentle word, a caring tone,
Can uplift and inspire, and make hearts feel at home.

Ya Rabb, guide us to be present and true,
Empathetic and kind, in all we do.
May our responses reflect love and respect,
And fulfil our rights, as Muslims, to earn Your pleasure and protection.

Our Prophet Muhammad (PBUH) taught us with grace,
"A kind word is a charity." (Sahih Bukhari)
May our words and actions be a blessing to share,
A source of comfort, strength, and inspiration to show we care.

In every interaction, may we choose to see,

The value in others, and the beauty in humanity.
May our kindness and compassion be a shining light,
Guiding us forward, through the darkness of night.

May Allah (SWT) bless our words, our hearts, and our deeds,
And make us a source of love, and a blessing to those in need.

"And the servants of the Most Merciful are those who walk upon the earth in sedateness and humility and when the ignorant address them [harshly], they say [words of] peace." (Quran 25:63)

May kindness bloom like wildflowers in every interaction, compassion overflow like a bountiful harvest from every heart, and peace whisper like a gentle stream through every word, reflecting the radiant beauty of our faith.

My Message to You

May whispers of love and compassion guide you to sprinkle kindness like fairy dust in every interaction. May your words be whispers that calm storms, gentle breezes that soothe hearts, and warm sunshine that uplifts souls. May Allah (SWT) bless your heart with empathy that understands, and peace that transcends. Ameen.

As We Conclude Part 4

As we gently close the pages of Part 4, "Poems of Reflection and Growth," may the whispers of these words remain in your heart, nurturing self-awareness, spiritual growth, and devotion. May the lessons learnt and reflections sparked by these poems guide you toward a deeper understanding of yourself and your faith, just as the Quran reminds us, "And indeed, with hardship comes ease." (Quran 94:5)

May our hearts overflow with compassion, kindness, and peace, like a garden that blooms in the desert. May Allah (SWT) guide us on this path, cultivating self-awareness, spiritual growth, and devotion. May we trust in His plan and wisdom, finding comfort in His mercy.

As we move forward to Part 5, "Self-Discovery and Healing," join me on this enchanting journey of spiritual exploration, discovery, and transformation. May Allah (SWT) bless us with hearts that overflow with hope, minds that shine with wisdom, and spirits that soar with peace and positivity. May our lives reflect the beauty and joy of our faith, and may our bond with one another be strengthened by empathy, compassion, and understanding.

Ameen.

PART 5
POEMS OF SELF-DISCOVERY AND HEALING
(PATH TO INNER PEACE)

Path to Inner Peace guides you on a journey of self-discovery, healing, and self-love, reminding you of the beauty and worth of the human soul.

Welcome to **Part 5** of my poetic journey,

"Poems of Self-Discovery and Healing."

As we twirl through life's winding paths, where petals of challenge and growth unfurl like a mesmerising dance, join me on this enchanting journey of self-discovery and healing. May the whispers of hope and resilience serenade us, and may the promise of ease that follows hardship be a gentle lullaby that rocks our souls to sleep. **"And indeed, with hardship comes ease."** (Quran 94:5)

Lessons Learnt and Takeaways
May these poems be a lantern guiding you to the treasure trove of your soul, where four precious gems await:

1. **Nurture Your Soul's Garden:**
   Like a garden that blooms with tender care, may you cultivate self-love and self-compassion, trusting in Allah's plan "**And your Lord has decreed that you not worship except Him, and to parents, good treatment...**" (Quran 17:23).

2. **Sunrise Serenity:**
   Like a sunrise that paints the sky with vibrant hues, may you find peace in Allah's creation, cultivating gratitude and wonder. "**And We have sent down blessed rain from the sky.**" (Quran 50:9)

3. **River of Forgiveness:**
   Like a river that flows effortlessly, may you let go of pain and hurt, embracing forgiveness and trust in Allah's wisdom. "**Let them pardon and forgive. Do you not love that Allah forgives you?**" (Quran 24:22)

4. **Masterpiece of Imperfections:**
   Like a masterpiece with unique brushstrokes, may you accept and love yourself, imperfections and all, trusting in Allah's plan. "**We will test you with some fear, hunger, and loss of wealth, lives, and crops. But give good news to those who are patient.**" (Quran 2:155)

May our journey be a celestial waltz, filled with self-discovery, healing, and the radiant light of faith. May our hearts overflow with peace, love, and compassion, and may we emerge from this journey with souls that shine like stars in the velvet night sky, twinkling with joy and wonder. Ameen.

May gentle whispers of self-compassion guide you to meet yourself where you are, embracing the beauty of your journey. May your heart overflow with trust in Allah's plan, and may your soul soar with the freedom of letting go. As you breathe in the beauty of the present, may you exhale the weight of worry, knowing the Allah (SWT) is always by your side...

"My Mind and Me"

In the warmth of my soul, I meet myself today,
With kindness, compassion, and love that never fades away.
I wrap myself in gentle care, and whisper words so true,
"You are enough, dear one, just as you are, in all you do."

The Quran's wisdom whispers, "And indeed, with hardship comes ease." (94:5)
A reminder that life's challenges will eventually bring release.
I let go of worries, of rushing to the finish line,
Trusting that what's meant for me is already mine, a divine design.

The stars align in my favour, a celestial promise so grand,
Guiding me through life's journey, with the Almighty's loving hand.
With every inhale, I welcome peace, serenity, and calm,
And as I exhale, slowly, I know Allah's presence will disarm.

All worries, all fears, all doubts, they fade away,
As I trust in the Almighty's plan, every step of the way.
So I'll reach for those stars, and breathe in deeply, too,
Knowing Allah's love and guidance will forever see me through.

May Allah's love envelop me, and guide me on my way,

And may I always remember, I am loved, every single day.

"And indeed, with hardship comes ease." (Quran 94:5)

May this ayah whisper secrets of hope and peace, reminding us that every challenge blooms with relief and ease. May our hearts overflow with trust in Allah's plan, and may our souls dance with the freedom of letting go.

My Message to You
May this poem be a gentle breeze that stirs your heart, inspiring you to cultivate self-love, self-compassion, and trust in Allah's guidance. May you find peace in His presence, and may your soul be nurtured by the knowledge that you are loved, more than words can say. May you meet yourself where you are, and may your journey be filled with serenity, calm, and the beauty of self-acceptance. Ameen.

May the gentle wisdom of the Quran guide us to cherish kindness to ourselves, embracing the divine love that resides within. May we awaken to the sacred right of self-care, nurturing our souls with compassion, peace, and harmony. As we journey inward, may we discover the beauty of self-love, and may our hearts overflow with the gentle touch of kindness and acceptance...

"A Love Letter to Myself: Be Kind to Yourself"

In the Quran's wisdom, a gentle reminder I find,
"And be kind to yourself." (17:23)
A love so divine.

Why do I forget this self-love so true?
Why do I neglect the care that's meant for me, too?
Society's expectations, a weight I've carried long,
A burden that's blinded me, to my own heartfelt song.

But now I awaken to a new dawn's light,
A realisation that self-care is my sacred right.
It's being present, in each moment I breathe,
Engaging with my thoughts, feelings, and surroundings, in harmony.

A simple act of reading, a book that brings me peace,
A moment to relax, reflect, recharge, and release.
In these quiet moments, I find my true self,
A sense of rejuvenation, a love that's wealth.

So I ask myself, dear one, what does self-love mean?
How do I prioritise, this love that's unseen?

Do I have non-negotiables that safeguard my soul?
How do I handle stress and find my heart's goal?

May I learn to love myself, exactly as I am,
A unique and beautiful creation, worthy of love's gentle hand.
Ya Rabb, Alhumdulilah, for blessings that abound,
May I cherish self-love and kindness that's profound.

May I strive to live by Your principles so true,
And prioritise self-care, as a love that shines through. Ameen.

"And lower to them the wing of humility out of mercy and say, 'My Lord, have mercy upon them as they brought me up [when I was] small.'" (Quran 17:24)

Like a soft breeze carrying the fragrance of rose petals, may this ayah whisper secrets of kindness and compassion, gently reminding us to cradle ourselves and others in mercy and love. May our hearts bloom with self-awareness, self-love, and tender kindness, spreading beauty and warmth wherever we go.

My Message to You
May this poem be a gentle guide, inspiring you to prioritise self-love, self-care, and kindness. May you let go of societal expectations, embracing your individuality and the beauty of your soul. May Allah (SWT) guide you towards a deeper understanding of self-care and love, and may your heart be filled with compassion, peace, and harmony. Ameen.

May the gentle touch of rain soothe your soul, and may the beauty of Allah's creation guide you to peace, serenity, and a deeper connection with the Divine. May the whispers of nature awaken your heart to the healing power of the natural world, and may you find solace in the majesty of Allah's design...

"Healing Rain"

Tears from the sky, a mercy so divine,
Healing rain, washing away my heart's confines.
In every drop, a blessing, reminders of Allah's care,
A soothing balm, for my soul, beyond compare.

In the Quran's words, "And We have sent down blessed rain from the sky." (50:9)
I find solace in this promise, a love that's always nigh.
As raindrops fall, like diamonds from above,
I feel Allah's presence, a love that's endless and pure.

My heart, once heavy, now lifted and free,
In the rhythm of the rain, I find serenity.
May this healing rain bring peace to my soul,
And remind me of Allah's love, making me whole.

May every drop be a blessing, a mercy, and a guide,
Leading me closer to Allah's heart, where love resides.

Ameen.

> "And We have sent down blessed rain from the sky." (Quran 50:9)

May this ayah whisper secrets of Allah's mercy and love, reminding us that every drop of rain brings life, nourishment, and rejuvenation. May our hearts overflow with gratitude for the natural world, and may we find peace and solace in the beauty of creation.

My Message to You

May this poem be a gentle breeze that stirs your soul, inspiring you to appreciate the wonder of the world around you. May you cultivate a deeper connection with Allah's love and wisdom, and may the beauty of creation guide you closer to His heart, where love resides. May you find peace, serenity, and joy in the natural world, and may it remind you of Allah's mercy and blessings. Ameen.

May the journey of growth and evolution be a radiant path, illuminated by the light of faith, wisdom, and spiritual insight. May we rise with purpose, and may our transformation be a testament to the beauty of Allah's guidance. As we strive to be the best version of ourselves, may we surround ourselves with those who inspire, uplift, and remind us of Allah's love and light...

"As You Evolve"

As you grow, as you rise
In faith, in wisdom, in spiritual eyes,
Take notice of those who rejoice with glee,
At the new version of you, a better you, they see.

Those who celebrate your growth, your shine,
Are the ones who'll uplift and be divine.
They're the ones who'll encourage and be kind,
And help you stay on track, on the path that's aligned.

In the Quran, Allah (SWT) says, "And indeed, you are of a great moral character." (Quran 68:4)
Strive to be the best, and let your character shine.

Surround yourself with those who inspire,
Who bring out the best, and help you reach higher,
Those who remind you of Allah's love and light,
And help you stay focused on the path that's right.

May Allah (SWT) guide us as we grow and evolve,
And may we surround ourselves with those who help us revolve,
Around the principles of faith, of love, and of light,
And may our evolution be a source of guidance and a beacon in the night. Ameen.

"And indeed, you are of a great moral character." (Quran 68:4)

May the petals of growth unfurl like tender rosebuds, gently revealing the radiant beauty of your soul. May your journey of evolution be a soulful waltz of faith, wisdom, and love, guided by the gentle whispers of Allah's heart, where every step is a symphony of trust and devotion.

My Message to You
May this poem be a tender breeze that nurtures your spirit, inspiring you to blossom into the best version of yourself. May you be surrounded by love, light, and the gentle guidance of those who uplift you. May your path be filled with wonder, and may your heart overflow with the joy of connecting with Allah's love and wisdom. Ameen.

May the gentle breeze of forgiveness soothe your soul, and may the warmth of love and mercy guide you to peace. May the whispers of Allah's heart remind you that forgiveness is a gift, a reflection of the divine love that resides within you...

"Forgiveness: The Best Form of Love"

With every breath, I let go of the pain,
And choose to forgive, with a heart that's not in vain.
For in forgiveness, I find peace, a love that's true,
A reflection of Allah's mercy, shining bright and new.

As I release the hurt, the weight that I've borne,
I feel the warmth of love that's been waiting to be born.
The Almighty's words echo, "Forgive, and you shall be forgiven." (Quran 24:22)
A promise of peace that my soul has been craving.

In this act of forgiveness, I find my heart's reprieve,
A chance to start anew, with a love that's meant to breathe.
All praises are due to Allah (SWT) for guiding me to this place,
Where love and forgiveness entwine, and fill my heart with space.

Here's to new beginnings, born of forgiveness, true
May my heart be filled with love and my spirit be renewed.
May Allah's mercy and love envelop me on my way,
And may forgiveness be the gift that I give each new day.

Ameen.

> **"Forgive, and you shall be forgiven."** (Quran 24:22)

Like a gentle morning dew that softly kisses the petals of our souls, may this ayah whisper secrets of peace and healing, reminding us that forgiveness is a divine balm that sets our hearts free, and may our spirits soar on the wings of love, compassion, and wisdom.

My Message to You

May this poem be a gentle breeze that stirs your heart, inspiring you to reflect on the transformative power of forgiveness. May you find peace, healing, and spiritual growth in the act of forgiveness, and may your life be a testament to the divine love and mercy that resides within you. May forgiveness be a guiding light on your journey, and may your heart be filled with the peace and serenity that comes from letting go. Ameen.

May the gentle whispers of Allah's love guide us to embrace our imperfections, and may the light of self-acceptance illuminate our path. May we find peace and healing in the knowledge that we are masterpieces, crafted with precision and love...

"Embracing My Broken Pieces"

In the gentle whispers of my soul, I hear a voice so true,
A reminder that I'm a masterpiece, crafted by Allah (SWT), anew.
With every breath, I'm woven with love, care, and might,
A unique tapestry, with threads of strength, shining so bright.

My broken pieces, though imperfect, tell a story so divine,
A testament to my resilience, and a heart that's truly mine.
As Allah (SWT) says, "We will test you with some fear, hunger, and loss of wealth, lives, and crops, but give good news to those who are patient." (Quran 2:155)

I'll not hide my imperfections, but instead, I'll embrace them.
With compassion, kindness, and love, I'll find my way to a peaceful place.
For in embracing my broken pieces,
I'll find true beauty, true strength, and true healing.

Ya Rabb, Alhumdulilah, for creating me with love and care,
For being patient with me and guiding me through life's joys and snares.
May You show me to love and accept myself, with all my flaws,

And may I walk with Your grace, knowing You're my Creator,
and You don't make mistakes, Subhanallah.
May I reflect on Your names, Al-Jabbar, Al-Qadir, Al-Latif,
The Repairer, The Powerful, The Gentle, guiding me through
life's journey and its shifts.
May I do that which pleases You, always, and may I be,
A reflection of Your love, compassion, and mercy, for all to see.
Ameen., Ya Rabb, Ameen.

"We will test you with some fear, hunger, and loss of wealth, lives, and crops. But give good news to those who are patient."
(Quran 2:155)

Like a seed that sprouts in the gentle rain, may this ayah nurture our souls, reminding us that life's challenges are opportunities for growth, and with patience, our roots of resilience will deepen, our stems of strength will rise, and our blooms of beauty will flourish.

My Message to You
May this poem be a gentle breeze that stirs your soul, inspiring you to reflect on your own resilience and strength. May you find the courage to accept your broken pieces with compassion, kindness, and love. May you walk with Allah's grace, knowing that You are a unique and beautiful creation, and may your heart overflow with the peace and healing that comes from self-acceptance. Ameen.

May the gentle whispers of Allah's love guide us through the darkness, and may the light of hope illuminate our path. May we find the courage to move forward, leaving heartache behind, and may our hearts be filled with the promise of new beginnings...

"Moving On"

Moving on, with heart and soul,
From shattered vows and love that's grown cold.
The pain endured, like autumn's fading light,
Yet, in the darkness, a new dawn takes flight.

With every step, we leave the heartache behind,
And find solace in the guidance of our Rabb's divine.
The weight of broken promises slowly starts to fade,
As we embark on a journey, where love and trust are remade.

The road ahead may seem uncertain and long,
But with faith as our compass, we'll find where we belong.
Our hearts, once broken, now heal with every stride,
As we move forward, side by side, with our Rabb as our guide.

May Allah's love and mercy envelop us on our way,
And may our hearts remain open to a brighter, newer day.

Ameen.

"And whoever relies upon Allah, then He is sufficient for him. Indeed, Allah will accomplish His purpose. Allah has already set for everything a decreed [extent]." (Quran 65:3)

May the soft whispers of trust gently guide us into the warm embrace of Allah's loving care, where every step is illuminated by the golden light of His divine plan, and every heart finds peaceful refuge in the ocean of His sufficient love.

My Message to You

May this poem be a soothing balm to your soul, reminding you that with every step, you can leave pain behind and find solace in the guidance of your Rabb. May you embark on a journey of healing and growth, and may Allah's love and mercy envelop you on your way to a brighter, newer day. Ameen.

A sprinkle of stardust, a dash of soul...
Welcome to "Embracing My True Self," where the magic of self-love, faith, and identity unfolds like a blooming garden of wonder. May these words be the gentle breeze that carries you to the shores of your own heart, where love, acceptance, and inner peace await...

"Embracing My True Self"

I once was lost, in the eyes of others' sight,
Judged by skin, by hair, by day and night.
Not Indian enough, not Coloured enough, I'd hear,
A mixed heritage, that brought me fear.

But then I realised, I'm more than just a face,
My heart beats strong, with a soul that's full of grace.
I am human, with love and dreams that shine,
Why must others define what's truly mine?

The world outside, with its expectations wide,
Tried to mould me, to fit into its stride.
But Allah's love showed me a different way,
I am enough, just as I am, every single day.

The Quran reminds us, "O mankind, indeed We have created you from male and female and made you peoples and tribes that you may know one another. Indeed, the most noble of you in the sight of Allah is the most righteous of you" (Quran 49:13).

Now I stand tall, with a heart that's free,
No longer bound by others' scrutiny.
I've come full circle, and I've learnt to see,
My worth, my value, in the eyes of my Creator's love, I'm me.

I celebrate every inch of my skin,
Every curve, every line, every part within.
I am a masterpiece, created with love and care,
A unique blend of cultures, beyond compare.

With a soul that shines, reflecting Allah's love,
I'll walk in confidence, sent from above.
Embracing my true self, with every step I take,
I'll find my strength in the love that Allah (SWT) makes.

With every step, I claim my space,
Embracing my identity, with a smile on my face.
No longer hiding, no longer afraid,
I'll shine my light and let my spirit sway.

My heart beats strong, with a soul that's free,
I'll dance to the rhythm of my own melody.
I'll celebrate my heritage with pride,
A mixed blessing, that makes me, me, inside.

In the eyes of Allah (SWT), I am seen,
A unique creation, with a story to be gleaned.
I'll hold on tight to my faith and my creed,
And find my strength in the words that I read.

So let the world, with all its strife,
I'll stand firm in my truth and thrive in life.
For I am me, and that's all that matters,

A child of love, with a heart that flatters.

"O mankind, indeed We have created you from male and female and made you peoples and tribes that you may know one another. Indeed, the most noble of you in the sight of Allah is the most righteous of you." (Quran 49:13)

Like a garden full of blooming flowers, each one distinct and beautiful, may this ayah remind us to cherish the diversity within and around us, embracing our true selves with all our unique petals, fragrances, and splendour.

My Message to You

May this poem be a gentle breeze that stirs your heart, inspiring you to embark on a journey of self-discovery and self-love. May it guide you to celebrate your individuality, and may your heart overflow with confidence, compassion, and acceptance for yourself and others. May Allah (SWT) guide us to be true to ourselves and to live with purpose, love, and kindness, Ameen.

In the gentle whispers of the Quran, we find a sacred reminder: to love and care for ourselves, just as we would tend to a precious garden. "Reflection on Self-Care and Self-Love" is a heartfelt invitation to embark on a journey of self-discovery, where we prioritise our own well-being and cultivate love for our unique selves...

"Reflection on Self-Care and Self-Love"

A gentle reminder, a sacred call
To love oneself, to hear the heart's whisper all
In a world that demands, we often forget
To nurture our souls, to let our spirits be set

The Quran's wisdom, a guiding light
"Be kind to yourself," a beacon in the night
Yet, we neglect, we prioritise others' needs,
Leaving our own hearts like withered seeds.

Let us unlearn the unhealthy ways
And cultivate love in each new day.
Self-care is presence, in every moment's breath
A book, a walk, a dua, a chance to rediscover depth.

Treasured moments to relax, reflect, recharge
To rejuvenate, to simply be, without a single charge
What does showing up for yourself mean?
Prioritise your heart, let self-love be seen.

You are worthy, uniquely crafted with love,
By the Divine Hands, sent from above

Ya Rabb, Alhumdulilah, for blessings so true
May we love ourselves, as You love us, anew.

Ameen., with love and duas, may our hearts be light.

"And be conscious of Allah; indeed, Allah is ever Knowing and Wise" (Quran).

Like a warm sunbeam gently touching our hearts, may this spirit of mindfulness remind us to nurture our inner light, cultivating self-care, self-love, and harmony, that we may shine brighter, living in perfect sync with ourselves and the world around us.

My Message to You
May this poem be a gentle breeze that stirs your heart, inspiring you to prioritise your own well-being and cultivate love for yourself. May it guide you to show up for yourself, listen to your heart's whispers, and overflow with self-compassion and self-acceptance. May Allah (SWT) guide us to care for ourselves, live with intention, and radiate love and kindness. Ameen.

Like a gentle dawn breaking on the horizon, the Quran's divine light illuminates our souls, whispering secrets of hope, faith, and resilience. May the verses of this poem be a soothing balm to your heart, reminding you of Allah's boundless love and mercy. As you read these words, may your spirit soar on the wings of faith, and may the Quran's transformative power touch your heart, filling your life with purpose, peace, and guidance...

"Al Quran, A Gift Divine"

In the treasure trove of existence, a gem beyond compare,
Lies the Quran, a gift from Allah (SWT), beyond measure or share.
Every letter, every word, every ayah, every surah, a masterpiece so fine,
Guidance from our Lord Supreme, a beacon that shines divine.

Within its sacred pages, stories of prophets unfold.
Trials, tribulations, and triumphs, lessons learnt, young and old.
From Adam (Alayhis Salaam), the Father of Humanity,
To Muhammad (Sallallahu Alayhi Wa Sallam), the Seal of Prophethood's dignity.

Their journeys, a testament to Allah's might,
A reminder of His power, mercy, and love, shining so bright.
Oh, believer, beware, for Allah (SWT) is the Controller, the Owner, the Supreme,
Fear Him, and follow His guidance, to avoid the fiery extremes.

No other book can ever compare to what lies within,
The Quran's wisdom, guidance, and truth forever win.
For in its pages, we find the secrets of the universe revealed,
A blueprint for living, a guide to paradise, our hearts and souls healed.

Learn to be thankful; learn to live life with purpose and grace.
Respect all living beings and follow the Quran's sacred pace.
Priceless lessons await if we only seek,
May we be wise and choose the path that's unique.

Embrace the Quran, embed its guidance in your heart,
Make it your life's worth, and never depart.
Who are we if we don't listen, if we don't follow the Quran's lead?
Lost souls, astray, without direction, in a world of need.

Let not Shaytan whisper deceit; let not his snares entwine.
Choose wisely, dear brother, dear sister, and align with the divine.
What have we to lose, what have we to gain?
Either we follow the Quran or succumb to Shaytan's snare and pain.

Jahannam or Jannah awaits; the choice is ours to make.
Trust in Allah (SWT), the Supreme, our Hero, our Everything, for our sake.
May Allah (SWT) guide us, protect us, and grant us wisdom's light,
To follow the Quran's guidance and walk the path that's right.

May its words be our solace, our comfort, our peace,
Our heart's eternal companion, our soul's release. Ameen.

"And indeed, it is a revelation from the Lord of the worlds."
(Quran 26:192)

May this divine whisper remind us of the Quran's gentle guidance, nurturing our souls like a soft morning breeze that awakens the flowers.

My Message to You

May this poem be a delicate petal that unfolds your heart, inviting you to cherish the Quran's wisdom and guidance. May its words be a soothing melody that resonates deep within you, inspiring you to dance with faith, sparkle with hope, and bloom with love. May Allah's gentle guidance illuminate your path, filling your life with wonder, peace, and joy, Ameen.

As We Conclude Part 5

As the petals of **Part 5, "Poems of Self-Discovery and Healing,"** gently close, may the fragrance of these words bloom in your heart, nurturing self-awareness, spiritual growth, and devotion like a garden kissed by morning dew. May Prophet Muhammad's (peace be upon him) gentle guidance remind us, **"He who knows himself, knows his Lord."** (Hadith, Narrated by Al-Bukhari), illuminating our path with the soft glow of wisdom and peace.

May our souls unfurl like desert roses, resilient and beautiful, as we trust in Allah's loving plan and wisdom. May our hearts overflow with compassion, kindness, and peace, like a garden that flourishes in the warm light of faith, spreading its fragrance far and wide.

As we embark on **Part 6, "Social Awareness and Justice,"** join me on this enchanting journey of spiritual exploration, discovery, and transformation. May Allah (SWT) bless us with hearts that dance with hope, minds that shine with wisdom, and spirits that soar with peace and positivity. May our lives reflect the beauty and joy of our faith, and may our bond with one another be strengthened by empathy, compassion, and understanding. Ameen.

PART 6
POEMS OF SOCIAL AWARENESS AND JUSTICE
(VOICES FOR CHANGE)

In Voices for Change, I speak out against injustice, advocating for compassion, kindness, and understanding, inspiring you to make a positive impact in the world.

Welcome to **Part 6** of my poetic journey,
"Poems of Social Awareness and Justice."

As we meander through life's intricate paths, we encounter challenges that test our faith, resilience, and hope. Join me on this soulful journey, where social awareness and justice unfold like petals of a flower. Through these poems, may you find the transformative power of standing up for justice and righteousness, guided by Islamic principles and emotional intelligence.

"O you who have believed, be persistently standing firm for Allah, witnesses in justice, and do not let the hatred of a people prevent you from being just." (Quran 5:8) May these words be a gentle breeze that inspires your soul, reminding you to stand firm in justice and righteousness.

Lessons Learnt and Takeaways

As you meander through these poems, may the gentle whispers of wisdom guide you, unfolding like rose petals in your heart. May you take away the following enchanting lessons:

1. **The Melody of Dua and Supplication:**
   Like a sweet serenade that reaches the heavens, may you prioritise dua and supplication, trusting in Allah's loving response. **"And your Lord says, 'Call upon Me; I will respond to you.'"** (Quran 40:60)

2. **A Beacon of Justice:**
   Like a radiant sunrise that chases away the night, may you be inspired to stand up against injustice, shining bright with compassion and courage. **"Whoever among you sees an evil, let him change it with his hand; and if he is not able to do so, then with his tongue; and if he is not able to do so, then with his heart."** (Hadith, Narrated by Muslim)

3. **Roots of Faith:**
   Like a majestic tree that stands tall, may you stay rooted in your faith and values, weathering life's storms with resilience and trust. **"And follow not the footsteps of Satan. Indeed, he is to you a clear enemy."** (Quran 2:168)

4. **The Fragrance of Kind Words:**
   Like a gentle breeze that carries the scent of roses, may you speak with kindness, truth, and love, spreading joy and positivity wherever you go. **"For indeed, good words are charity."** (Quran 2:177)

May our journey be a celestial dance, illuminated by the radiant light of faith, guiding us to stand tall for justice and righteousness. May our hearts overflow with compassion, kindness, and love, like a garden bursting with vibrant blooms. May our souls sparkle like diamonds in the sunlight, and may we emerge from this journey shining brightly, like stars that twinkle in the velvet night sky. Ameen.

A whispered dua on the winds of dawn, this poem carries the scent of gratitude and longing. May the resilience of Gaza's people be a beacon of hope, and may Allah's mercy envelop those who suffer. Let us lift our voices in supplication, seeking guidance and relief, as we strive to serve our Lord with hearts full of love and devotion...

"A Prayer for the People of Gaza"

Ya Rabb, Alhumdulilah, for each new day's light,
We praise Your wisdom in the darkest of nights.
The people of Gaza, a testament to faith's might,
Teaching us righteousness, in the face of endless fight.

Their resilience inspires; their courage in the face
Of calamity and hardship, a lesson in faith's sacred space.
We're grateful for these lessons, though our hearts ache with pain;
We know that Your methods, though mysterious, are never in vain.

You're the Best of Planners, the King of Kings above,
All-Knowing, All-Hearing, and All-Seeing, in boundless love.
Most Merciful, All-Forgiving, yet severe in punishment's sway.
We tremble with reverence, in awe of Your majestic way.

May Your mercy envelop the people of Gaza's plight,
And all believers facing catastrophes in this fleeting light.
May we, as the Ummah of our Beloved Prophet's Muhammad's (PBUH) guide,
Strive to put You first, in every step, with hearts full of pride.

May we serve You well, and do that which pleases Your heart,
May our actions be a reflection of our love for You, never to depart.
Subhanallah, we surrender to Your divine will and might,
Ya Rabb, have mercy on us, and guide us through the darkest night.

Ameen.

"And He [Allah] is the One who has created the heavens and the earth with truth, and the day He says, 'Be,' and it is." (Surah Al-Furqan, verse 2)

May this divine whisper remind us of Allah's majestic power, nurturing our trust like a gentle stream that quenches our soul's thirst, and soothing our hearts like a warm breeze on a summer day.

My Message to You
May this poem be a delicate feather that tickles your soul, inviting you to soar on the wings of dua and supplication like a bird riding the thermals of dawn. May its words be a gentle lullaby that rocks your heart, singing a melody of trust in Allah's wisdom, mercy, and justice, like a child snuggled in the arms of love. May Allah's

gentle guidance illuminate your path with stardust, filling your life with wonder that awes, peace that calms, and joy that overflows. Ameen.

A whispered cry on the winds of justice, this poem carries the heartbeat of courage and conviction. May the voices of the oppressed be a call to action, and may Allah's guidance illuminate our path. Let us stand together in solidarity, seeking to uplift the downtrodden and striving to serve our Lord with hearts full of compassion and love...

"When Genocide Becomes a Memory"

When genocide becomes a memory...
Etched in history's sombre symphony,
We're reminded of the lives lost, the pain and the strife,
A tragedy that befell a human life.

Be afraid, be very afraid, for we all must face,
The consequences of our actions. In this sacred,sacred space,
We'll answer for the role we played.
In their story, their plight, did we stand idly by, or shine a light?

The weight of silence, the burden of inaction,
Will haunt us, like a ghostly reaction,
For we're all accountable for the lives we could've saved,
The voices we could've amplified, the justice we could've craved.

So let us remember the lives that were lost,
And honour their memory, with a commitment to the cost,
Of standing up against injustice and hate,
And being the voice that echoes their fate.

Ameen.

> "Whoever kills a person, it is as if he has killed all of humanity; and whoever saves a person, it is as if he has saved all of humanity." (Quran 5:32)

This ayah whispers secrets of compassion and care, reminding us that every life is a precious garden, worthy of protection and love. It stirs our souls to tend to one another, to stand against the winds of injustice, and to be a shelter from the storms of violence.

My Message to You

May this poem be a gentle breeze that carries the whispers of the past, reminding us to honour the lives lost, and to stand up against injustice and hate. May you be a voice for the voiceless, a refuge for the vulnerable, and a beacon of hope in the darkest corners. May your heart overflow with compassion, your spirit be guided by justice, and your actions reflect the beauty of humanity. Ameen.

Like a gentle stream that flows with serene purpose, this poem whispers reminders to anchor your heart in faith and lets the gentle breeze of spiritual guidance carry you through life's turbulent waters. May its words be a soft whisper in your ear, guiding you to prioritise your soul's nourishment and to bloom with virtue in the garden of life...

"Don't Be Swayed: Halaal/Haram"

In a world where norms are swayed,
And right and wrong are often conveyed,
Remember, Haram is Haram, no matter the crowd,
And Halaal is Halaal, even when you stand proud.

When all around you seem to indulge and delight,
In forbidden pleasures that shine with worldly light,
Don't be swayed by the masses or the temporary thrill,
For in the end, it's your soul that will face the ultimate bill.

And when you're the only one who chooses the righteous path,
And the world around you seems to mock and laugh,
Remember, your Lord is watching, and your deeds are being weighed,
And the reward of the Akhirah far surpasses the fleeting joys of this worldly stage.

So choose your path wisely, dear believer, choose with care,
For the temptations of this world are but a snare,
To distract you from the truth and the ultimate prize,
Of Jannah's bliss, and Allah's pleasure, that opens wide the gates of paradise.

May Allah (SWT) guide us on the straight path and give us the strength.
To resist the temptations and hold fast to our faith's length,

Ameen.

"And follow not the footsteps of Satan. Indeed, he is to you a clear enemy." (Quran 2:168)

This ayah whispers warnings of shadowy whispers, reminding us to beware the sly footsteps of Shaytan, who seeks to lead us down winding paths. May its words be a gentle breeze that guides you to anchor your heart in faith, to prioritise your soul's nourishment, and to walk the radiant path of righteousness.

My Message to You
May this poem be a soft light on your journey, illuminating the straight path and guiding you to make choices that bloom with virtue. May you find strength in Allah's guidance, and may your heart overflow with peace, wisdom, and compassion. Ameen.

Like delicate petals carried on the breeze, our words hold the power to nurture or wound. This poem whispers gentle truths about the art of speaking from the heart, and the tender touch of kindness that can heal or harm. May its words guide you to craft a garden of kindness with every phrase, and to speak with love that uplifts and inspires...

"Words Are Energy, Choose Yours Wisely"

In the Quran, Allah (SWT) reminds us to speak kindly,
"For indeed, good words are charity." (Quran 2:177)
Our words have power, to heal or to harm,
To build or to break, to disarm.

Choose your words wisely, with care and with thought,
For they can bring blessings, or cause hearts to be caught.
Speak truth, speak kindness, speak love and speak light,
For in doing so, you'll bring peace to the night.

As the Prophet (PBUH) said, "Verily, a servant may utter a word, not realising its implications,
And because of it, he may fall into the Hellfire." (Bukhari)
May our words be a source of guidance, mercy, and peace,
And may Allah (SWT) forgive us for any words that may cause unease.

Ameen.

"For indeed, good words are charity" (Quran 2:177), a gentle breeze that carries the fragrance of kindness. And yet, **"Verily, a servant may utter a word, not realising its implications, and because of it, he may fall into the Hellfire"** (Bukhari), a solemn reminder to tend to our words like a gardener tends to a delicate bloom.

My Message to You

May this poem be a soft whisper in your ear, guiding you to cultivate a garden of kindness with every phrase, and to speak with love that uplifts and inspires. May your words be a source of healing, guidance, and peace, and may your voice be a melody of compassion and empathy. Ameen.

Like a delicate petal that unfurls with gentle care, respect is a priceless gift that can bloom in the most unexpected ways. This poem whispers secrets of harmony and kindness, reminding us that respect is a radiant light that can illuminate even the darkest corners of our lives. May its words guide you to sprinkle respect like stardust, freely and without condition, and to trust that goodness will unfold like a blooming garden...

"Respect: A Priceless Gift"

Respect, oh respect, to elders, parents, children, family,
And friends, a virtue that's essential, until the very end.
They say respect is earned, not given freely,
But I say, give it freely, and watch how life unfolds with glee.

Learn to set healthy boundaries, trust the process,
And see the rewards of respect, in harmony.
When someone's rude, don't be the same.
My mum's wise words echo: "Show them the other cheek, and treat them with respect, all the same."

It wasn't easy, but I tried until I realised,
I'd lost myself, and my identity compromised.
I treated others as they treated me,
But didn't like who I became, and the friends I lost, tragically.

A lesson learnt, a space I won't revisit,
Now, I'm rebuilding and rediscovering my true self's bliss.
Always show respect, for Allah's opinion matters most.
To all, come what may, respect is a priceless gift, forever to boast.

It costs nothing to show respect, yet its value is immense,
Attracting goodness and expanding our universe with elegance.

So, do what's right, show respect, and watch life unfold,
A priceless gift from our One True Rabb, forever to hold.

"And speak to people kindly..." (Quran 2:83)

A gentle melody that echoes through the chambers of our hearts. May this poem be a soft breeze that carries the fragrance of respect and kindness, reminding us to tend to our words like a gardener tends to a blooming garden.

My Message to You
May this poem inspire you to sprinkle kindness like rose petals and to speak with a voice that soothes the soul. May respect be your guiding light, and may your interactions be infused with empathy, compassion, and love. May your words be a balm to those who need it most, and may your heart overflow with peace and goodness. Ameen.

Like a wildflower that blooms in its own sweet time, this poem whispers secrets of authenticity and courage. May its words guide you to unfurl your petals, to show up as you are, and to shine with the radiant light of your true self. May you blossom into the most vibrant version of you, and may your presence be a gift to the world...

"Show up Authentically"

Show up, I say, show up authentically,
No matter who you are, just show up and be.
Show up for your Rabb; show up for yourself;
Show up for others; just show up, and let your spirit breathe.

Show up, no matter what may come your way,
Listen, learn, grow, and heal every single day.
Evolve into the best version of yourself,
The one you've been born to be, with purpose and wealth.

Show up, just show up, it's a commitment to yourself,
To be present, to be mindful, and to live life on your own shelf.
Show up, show up, and be, don't hide or pretend.
You are enough, just as you are, your true self to amend.

"Verily, Allah does not look at your figures, nor at your attire, but He looks at your hearts and accomplishments" (Hadith, narrated by Muslim)

A gentle reminder that the beauty of the soul outshines the external. May this poem be a soft whisper in your ear, guiding you to tend to your heart like a gardener tends to a blooming garden.

My Message to You
May you unfurl your petals, embracing your true self with courage and vulnerability. May you trust in the divine plan, knowing that you are enough, just as you are. May your heart overflow with self-acceptance, mindfulness, and spiritual growth, and may your authenticity be a beacon of light in a world that celebrates uniqueness. Ameen.

Kindness is the language that the deaf can hear and the blind can see. May this poem be a gentle melody that whispers the beauty of compassion, reminding us that kindness is a gift that can be given without words, yet speaks volumes to the soul...

"Treat Others with Kindness"

What does it cost to treat others with kindness, I ask?
Surely, you know kindness makes us who we are, at last.
So share your kindness and spread the love,
It costs nothing to show who you truly are, from above.

Don't judge others, just be kind, it's true,
Whether they're rich or poor, it doesn't matter to you.
A few words or acts of kindness to go around
Will brighten up your day, beyond compare, without a sound.

A feeling that's given for all to share,
So be kind, I say, be kind, humanity, show you care.
Be kind to each other and set yourself free.
In kindness, we find love, and that's the key.

> "Kindness is a mark of faith, and whoever is not kind has no faith." (Hadith, narrated by Muslim)

A gentle reminder that compassion is the heartbeat of spirituality. May this poem be a soft breeze that carries the fragrance of kindness, inspiring you to tend to the gardens of your heart and nurture the blooms of empathy and love.

My Message to You
May you sprinkle kindness like rose petals on the path of life, and may your heart overflow with compassion and warmth. May you embody the gentle art of kindness, and may your presence be a balm to those who need it most. May your life be a testament to the transformative power of love and kindness. Ameen.

Like a sunbeam that bursts through the clouds, the gift of giving shines bright, illuminating hearts and spreading joy. May these words be a gentle reminder of the divine art of kindness, and may they inspire you to sprinkle love and compassion like rose petals on the path of life. As you read these lines, may your heart overflow with the sweetness of generosity and the warmth of giving...

"Gift of Giving, A Blessing Divine"

Ya Rabb, Alhumdulilah, for the gift of giving true,
May we make a difference in all we do.
A smile, a hug, a listening ear,
May our kindness be genuine, and our hearts be clear.

May we never underestimate the impact of a small deed,
On someone's self-esteem, and their heart's need.
For kindness is a sunnah that costs nothing to share,
Yet its value is priceless, beyond compare.

May today bring us joy in being kind and true,
May we cherish these moments and make them shine through.
For what we give to others, always finds its way back,
A lesson from our beloved Rabb, a priceless gift to unpack.

Subhanallah... Allah-u-Akbar...
Ameen.

"And be kind to the believers who follow you." (Quran 26:215)

A divine whisper that echoes the beauty of compassion. May this poem be a gentle melody that whispers the sweetness of kindness, inspiring you to tend to the gardens of your heart and nurture the blooms of generosity and love.

My Message to You
May you sprinkle kindness like rose petals on the path of life, and may your heart overflow with compassion and warmth. May you embody the gentle art of giving, and may your presence be a balm to those who need it most. May your life be a testament to the transformative power of love, kindness, and generosity. Ameen.

Like a sunrise that paints the sky with vibrant hues, a smile can illuminate the world, spreading joy and positivity wherever it goes. May this poem be a gentle reminder of the transformative power of self-love, self-care, and smiling, and may it inspire you to unlock the radiant light within you. As you read these words, may your heart overflow with compassion, kindness, and love for yourself and others...

"Smile, It's a Sunnah"

Oh, smile, beautiful being, smile!
Show us that radiant smile that brightens our day.
Smiling is a Sunnah, a blessing from above,
Spoken by our Beloved Prophet Muhammad (PBUH), a treasure of love.

Smile and turn that frown around,
Feel how it illuminates your path, without a sound.
Eliminating negativity as you walk along,
Attracting positivity, like a sweet, sweet song.

Your energy will surely return, lifting you high,
In ways you may not comprehend, but feel in your heart's eye.
So turn that frown upside down, and feel the delight,
A sense of joy that's been waiting, shining with all its might.

Delight that fills your heart, emotions that never fade,
Lifting your spirits, as you move forward, unafraid.
Smile, beautifully, smile lovely, show the world your light,
Welcome a smile in return, and watch how it fills the gap tonight.

Smile, it's a Sunnah, a priceless gift from Allah (SWT) above,
A treasure to cherish, a blessing of endless love.

May your smile be a beacon of hope, a ray of sunshine bright,
May it illuminate your path and guide you through life's plight.

"Smiling in the face of your brother is charity" (Hadith, narrated by Tirmidhi)

A precious gem that sparkles with kindness. May this poem be a soft breeze that carries the fragrance of joy, reminding you that a smile is a gift that can brighten the world and earn rewards in the hereafter.

My Message to You

May your smile be a ray of sunshine that illuminates the path of others, spreading joy and positivity wherever you go. May you embody the radiant light of kindness, and may your presence be a balm to those who need it most. May your life be a testament to the transformative power of smiling, and may you radiate love and kindness to all those around you. Ameen.

Like a sunrise that bursts through the morning dew, may this poem awaken your heart to the needs of those around you and inspire you to make a positive impact. May the gentle whispers of compassion and kindness guide you to look beyond yourself and share your love with the world. As you read these words, may your spirit be stirred to make a difference, starting today...

"Living in the Dark"

We live in communities, oblivious to the pain,
Blindsided by our own lives, judging from a distance, in vain.
Who are we to judge what we see?
Isn't judgment Allah's right, exclusively?

Our Prophet Muhammad (PBUH) taught us to look below,
To see the struggles of those less privileged, and to grow.
Not to compare ourselves to those above,
But to humble ourselves, and show compassion, with endless love.

Do you know what's happening in your community?
Or do you prefer to walk blindly, pretending not to see?
Look closely, pay attention, for things are at play,
Communities crying out, lost and astray.

How do we choose to be so oblivious?
Time to wake up, feel the breeze, and bring change, please.
Our Rabb desires our kindness and care,
Even small acts, consistently done, show we truly care.

No deed goes unnoticed, especially from the heart,
Our Rabb smiles, though we may not see, from the very start.
Use your gifts, expand, and lend a hand,

Helping others, you'll find, sets your own soul free to stand.

In the footsteps of our Prophet, let's strive to be
Compassionate, humble, and kind, for all to see.
Let's look to those less privileged and grow.
For in their struggles, we find our own growth.

Now, go out and make a difference, do your best,
Share your kindness, compassion, and love, and pass the test.
Remember, every small act counts, every smile, every tear,
Go out and make a difference, and bring joy, year after year!

"And indeed, you are of a great moral character" (Quran 68:4)

This ayah is a divine affirmation that shines like a star in the night sky, guiding us towards kindness, compassion, and empathy. May this poem be a gentle breeze that carries the fragrance of goodness, inspiring you to spread love, kindness, and positivity wherever you go.

My Message to You
May your heart overflow with compassion, kindness, and empathy, and may your actions be a reflection of your beautiful

character. May you be guided to look beyond yourself and lend a hand to those in need, and may your presence be a balm to those who need it most. May Allah (SWT) bless you with the wisdom to make a positive impact, and may your life be a testament to the transformative power of kindness and love. Ameen.

As We Conclude Part 6

As the petals of **Part 6** unfold like a garden of **social awareness and justice,** may the sweet fragrance of these poems linger, inspiring you to bloom into a radiant force for positive change. May the Prophetic words, **"The best of people are those who are most beneficial to others"** (Hadith, Narrated by Al-Bukhari), be the gentle breeze that guides you towards a path of kindness, compassion, and justice.

As we step into the enchanting realm of **Part 7, "Remembrance and Gratitude,"** may the celestial music of spirituality envelop you, nurturing your heart and soul with the harmony of divine love. May the hidden treasures of the human experience be revealed to you, guiding you towards healing, inspiration, and growth.

Ya Rabb, guide us on this mystical journey, we pray. May our hearts be infused with the nectar of empathy, compassion, and faith, and may our words and actions be a shining star of hope and guidance for others. Ameen.

Join me on this final journey, as we bask in the luminous glow of remembrance and gratitude, allowing its gentle whispers to transform our lives, and may our souls be forever changed, like a masterpiece of divine art.

PART 7
POEMS OF REMEMBRANCE AND GRATITUDE
(GRATITUDE AND PRAISE)

In Gratitude and Praise, I express heartfelt gratitude for the blessings of life, the beauty of nature, and the guidance of faith, celebrating the human experience and the divine presence in our lives.

Welcome to **Part 7** of my poetic journey,

" Poems of Remembrance and Gratitude."

As the morning sun rises over the horizon of our hearts, may the warmth of remembrance and gratitude awaken us to the blessings and wisdom that Allah (SWT) has bestowed upon us. Join me on this poetic journey, where the fragrance of Islamic principles and emotional intelligence intertwines with the beauty of human experience, illuminating the path to guidance, healing, and inspiration.

Lessons Learnt and Takeaways
As you wander through these poems, may you discover hidden treasures that inspire you to:

1. **Grateful Heart:**
   Cultivate gratitude and remembrance, recognising the blessings and wisdom that Allah (SWT) has bestowed upon us. "**And [remember] when your Lord proclaimed, 'If you are grateful, I will surely increase you in favour...'**" (Quran 14:7)

2. **Mirror of Authenticity:**
   Strive to cultivate self-awareness, authenticity, and vulnerability, recognising that these qualities are essential for personal growth and spiritual development. "**And be truthful, for truthfulness leads to righteousness.**" (Quran 19:76)

3. **Wings of Compassion:**
   Recognise the transformative power of kindness and compassion, and may we strive to embody these qualities in our interactions with others. "**Kindness is a mark of faith, and whoever is not kind has no faith.**" (Hadith, Narrated by Muslim)

4. **Nurturing Bonds:**
   Cherish and nurture our relationships with family and community, recognising the importance of these bonds in our lives. "**And We have honoured the children of Adam.**" (Quran 17:70)

5. **Path of Purpose:**
   Strive to live a life guided by purpose, values, and faith, recognising that this is the key to a life of meaning, fulfilment, and joy. **"The happiest of people is the one who is guided to a life of purpose."** (Hadith, Narrated by Ibn Majah)

May our journey be a celestial dance, filled with peace, love, and a deeper connection with our Rabb. May our hearts be filled with wonder, awe, and gratitude, and may our lives be a reflection of the beauty and kindness that emanates from our souls. Ameen.

Like a sunrise that paints the sky with hues of gold, may this poem illuminate the path to spiritual growth and guidance. May the gentle whispers of wisdom stir your soul, and may the love of our Rabb envelop you in warmth and peace. As you read these words, may your heart overflow with devotion, and may your spirit soar on wings of faith and trust...

"A Heart's Awakening"

In whispers of wisdom, I heard it said,
"It was Allah (SWT) who chose me, not I who chose the way ahead."
A truth that resonated deep within my soul,
Guiding me home, to a love that made me whole.

The journey's twists and turns, the search for peace,
Led me to Islam's door, where love and joy release.
Thirty-five years of devotion, of trials and of strife,
Yet in those words, I found the essence of life.

I bear witness now, with heart and soul,
"La ilaha illallah, Muhammadur Rasulullah," my heart's goal.
A declaration of faith, a promise to abide,
Submitting to Allah (SWT), with love, I'll reside.

A void within my heart, a space so vast and wide,
Longing for connection, for a love to abide.
And then I felt it, a warmth that spread like light,
Allah's love embracing me, banishing the dark of night.

My heart overflows with gratitude, my soul takes flight,
In praise of Allah (SWT), my Creator, my Guiding Light.

Alhumdulilah, Subhanallah, Allahu Akbar, I proclaim,
My love, my thanks, my surrender, in joy and in His name.

May my heart remain pure, my spirit stay aflame,
Serving Him with love, until we meet again.
In Jannah's gardens, where peace and love entwine,
I'll thank Him forever for choosing me, for making me mine.
Ameen.

"And whoever relies upon Allah, then He is sufficient for him."
(Quran 65:3)

This ayah whispers sweet melodies of trust and surrender, reminding us that Allah's guidance is the soft luminescence of a thousand fireflies on a summer night, illuminating our path with gentle certainty, guiding us home to the warmth of His love, where the stars of faith twinkle like diamonds in the velvet sky.

My Message to You
May this poem be a gentle breeze that stirs your soul, guiding you to the gardens of faith, where love blooms like a rose in full splendour, and devotion takes flight on the wings of a butterfly. May it whisper secrets of trust, surrender, and peace, and may

your heart overflow with gratitude like a fountain of sweet perfume, your spirit dance with joy like a child in a field of wildflowers, and your soul find solace in the divine like a bird finding its nest. Ameen.

Like a gentle breeze that carries the sweet scent of rose petals, our love story unfolds in the garden of life, nurtured by the divine guidance of Allah (SWT). In this poetic expression of devotion, may our hearts beat as one, and may our love be a reflection of the beauty and mercy that emanates from the heavens...

"Alhumdulillah, for My Life Partner, Best Friend and Love"

My soulmate, my everything, my love so true,
You're the rhythm that makes my heart sing anew.
In your eyes, my heart finds a home, a peaceful nest,
With you, my love, I'm forever blessed.

But there's something you should know, something that's clear,
Allah (SWT) occupies the centre of my heart, and always will be near.
He's the One who guides me, who loves me more than all;
My love for Him is unwavering, standing tall.

I hope you understand, my love, my heart's desire,
To serve Allah (SWT), to love Him, with every burning fire.
You're my partner, my friend, my confidant, my guide.
Together we'll walk the path, side by side.

Allah's wisdom brought us together in a union so divine,
Alhumdulilah, for this gift, that's forever intertwined.
You're my best friend, my partner, my forever love,
In your arms I find solace, sent from above.

So here's to our love, our journey, and our hearts beating as one,
May Allah (SWT) continue to bless us and guide us beneath the sun.
I love you more with each breath, each moment we share,
Forever grateful for you, my love, my soulmate, my everything.
Beyond compare.

Ameen.

"Among His signs is that He created for you mates from among yourselves, that you may dwell in tranquillity with them, and He has put love and mercy between your hearts. Verily in that are signs for those who reflect." (Quran 30:21)

Like a delicate rose blooming in the garden of love, this ayah reminds us that marriage is a beautiful sign of Allah's (SWT) wisdom and creation. May the gentle whispers of love, mercy, and tranquillity guide us in nurturing our relationships, and may our bond with our partner be a reflection of the divine love that emanates from the heavens.

My Message to You

May this poem be a soft breeze that carries the fragrance of love, kindness, and gratitude, inspiring you to cultivate a deeper connection with your partner and with Allah (SWT). May your heart overflow with devotion, and may your relationship be a sanctuary of peace, love, and spiritual growth. Ameen.

Like a morning sunrise that paints the sky with hues of gold, may our lives be illuminated with purpose and meaning. May our souls be guided by the divine wisdom of the Quran, and may our hearts be filled with the warmth of gratitude and love...

"My Divine Purpose"

A purpose-driven soul, a heart aflame,
Guided by Quranic wisdom, I know my name.
"And Allah (SWT) has created you for a purpose," I'm told,
A divine calling, a life to unfold.

With every breath, I'm humbled and grateful too,
For the gift of existence, and all that I can do.
Subhanallah, I marvel at the beauty and might,
Of a life filled with purpose, shining with delight.

Ya Rabb, Alhumdulilah, for every blessing I've known,
For the chance to serve others and make a difference shown.
May I continue to please You, dear Allah (SWT), every day,
And may my heart remain pure, in every single way.

May we flourish and bloom into the best versions of ourselves,
Guided by Your wisdom and surrounded by Your wealth.
And for those searching for purpose, may You show the way,
Granting strength and guidance, every step of the day.

Ameen., with love and duas, I pray and I hope,
May our lives be a reflection of Your divine scope.
Your humble servant, I remain, forever grateful and true,
To the purpose You've given me, and the life I live anew.

"And Allah has created you for a purpose."

This gentle reminder whispers to our souls that we are here for a reason, a purpose that only we can fulfil. May we listen to the whispers of our hearts and follow the guidance of our Rabb.

My Message to You
May this poem be a soft breeze that carries the fragrance of purpose and meaning into your life. May you be guided by the wisdom of the Quran, and may your heart be filled with gratitude and love for the blessings in your life. May you walk in the light of your divine purpose, and may your life be a reflection of the beauty and love that emanates from your Rabb. Ameen.

Like a gentle morning dew that tenderly touches the petals of our souls, may we find peace and solace in the wisdom of Allah's guidance. May our hearts be filled with gratitude and trust, as we navigate the journey of life...

"Alhumdulillah"

All praises rise, to the Almighty's throne,
For every blessing and every trial known.
In adversity's darkness, we search for the light,
And find solace in Allah's wisdom, guiding us through the night.

"No remover of it," the Quran's words proclaim,
Yet in submission, we find peace, and a heart that's not in pain.
For Allah's will is perfect; His plan divine and just,
We trust in His goodness and surrender to His trust.

And when good fortune smiles and blessings abound,
We accept with gratitude, and a heart that's turned around.
For Allah (SWT) is over all things, competent and wise,
We praise Him in every state, with a heart full of surprise.

Subhanallah, we surrender to Your divine decree,
And find peace in Your wisdom, for all eternity.

Ameen.

"And if Allah touches you with adversity , none can remove it but He; and if He touches you with good, then he is able to do all things." (Quran 6:17)

This Quranic reminder whispers to our souls that in times of adversity, we find solace in Allah's wisdom and guidance. May we trust in His perfect plan and find peace in His divine decree.

My Message to You

May this poem be a soft breeze that carries the fragrance of peace and trust into your heart. May you find solace in the wisdom of Allah's guidance, and may your heart be filled with gratitude and love for the blessings in your life. May you walk in the light of faith and trust, and may your life be a reflection of the beauty and wisdom that emanates from your Creator. Ameen.

In the garden of prophetic guidance, Prophet Muhammad (PBUH) is a blooming rose that fills the air with the fragrance of compassion, humility, and love. May his teachings be a source of inspiration and guidance for us, and may our lives be a reflection of the beauty and wisdom that emanate from his noble character...

"Our Beloved Prophet Muhammad (PBUH)"

In the realm of existence, where souls take flight,
Our beloved Prophet Muhammad (PBUH) shines with radiant light.
A creation of Allah (SWT), with a purpose so divine,
A messenger of mercy, with a heart so expansive and sublime.

With every breath, he embodied the Quran's sacred truth,
A living manifestation of Allah (SWT) wisdom and infinite youth.
His footsteps, guidance, for all humanity to tread,
A path of righteousness, where love and compassion are lavishly spread.

In his eyes, a reflection of Allah's boundless majesty,
A window to the divine, where hearts find their sacred ecstasy.
His smile, a brilliant beam of hope, and joy, and light,
Illuminating the journey through life's darkest, most trying night.

With every word he spoke, a treasure of wisdom was revealed,
A gift from Allah (SWT) to humanity, so precious and truly concealed.
His teachings, a balm to heal the wounds of the soul,

A reminder of Allah's love that makes us whole.

In his humility, we find a lesson to humbly embrace,
A quality of character that brings us to our knees in sacred praise.
His compassion, a shelter for the weak and the strong,
A refuge from life's storms, where hearts can safely belong.

Oh, our beloved Prophet, Muhammad, peace be upon him,
A treasure, so precious, a gift, so divine, and eternally sublime.
May our hearts be filled with love and reverence for thee,
And may our lives be guided by the light of thy radiant prophecy.

Ya Rabb, Alhumdulilah, for the gift of our beloved Prophet,
A blessing, so immense, a treasure, so rare, and uniquely bestowed.
May we cherish his teachings and follow his noble way,
And may our souls be nourished by the light of his radiant day.
Ameen.

"Indeed, in the Messenger of Allah, you have a good example to follow for him who hopes in Allah and the Last Day and remembers Allah much." (Quran 33:21)

Like a shining star that guides us through the night, Prophet Muhammad's (PBUH) life and teachings illuminate the path of righteousness. May his noble example be a gentle breeze that carries the fragrance of compassion, humility, and love into our hearts. May we follow his guidance and teachings, and may our lives be a reflection of the beauty and wisdom that emanate from his prophetic legacy.

My Message to You
May this poem be a soft whisper that awakens your soul to the beauty of Prophet Muhammad's (PBUH) character and teachings. May you be inspired to walk in his footsteps, and may your heart be filled with love, compassion, and guidance. Ameen.

In the symphony of life, gratitude is the melody that resonates in our hearts, praising Allah (SWT) for the harmony of faith, guidance, and love. May our words be a gentle breeze that carries the fragrance of thankfulness, and may our lives be a reflection of the beauty and wisdom that emanate from our Rabb...

"Gratitude"

Ya Rabb, Alhumdulilah, shukran for another day,
To see, to breathe, to live, and to pray.
Shukran for Your mercy, forgiveness, and guidance true,
For protecting us from harm, and seeing us through.

We thank You for our Prophet, Muhammad, peace be upon him,
Our guide, our teacher, our shining example to win.
He taught us Your principles, as revealed in the Quran's light,
And showed us how to live, with faith, with love, with all our might.

Shukran to Him for teaching us to worship You alone,
To prostrate, to pray, and to make our hearts Your throne.
Shukran for showing us righteousness, piety, and the way
To treat all living beings with kindness, every single day.

May we make You proud, every moment, every day,
Ya Rabb, use me as Your humble servant, in a small way.
May my poetry be a source of comfort, of light,
To guide those seeking a way out of darkness, into Your loving sight.

Subhanallah, may Your name be glorified, forevermore.

May our hearts be filled with love, and our souls be nourished once more.

Ameen.

"And whatever blessings you have, they are from Allah" (Quran 16:53)

Like a garden blooming with vibrant flowers, our lives are filled with blessings from Allah (SWT). May gratitude be the sunshine that nourishes our souls, and may our hearts be filled with thankfulness for the gifts of faith, love, and guidance.

My Message to You
May this poem be a gentle reminder to count your blessings, and may your heart be filled with joy and gratitude for the precious gifts in your life. May you walk in the light of faith and guidance, and may your words and actions spread love, comfort, and peace to those around you. Ameen.

As the final pages turn, the curtain lifts, and the beauty of Islam takes centre stage. Let's savour the sweetness of faith, like a whispered secret in the stillness of the night. May its gentle whispers guide us home, to a heart that's full of love and a soul that's at peace…

"The Beauty of Islam"

Where does one start to describe its charm?
A divine light guides me as I write from the heart.
Some may think it's endless dua, or salah's fivefold might,
Or Hajj and Umrah's sacred journeys, through day and night.

But alas, dear friends, this is not the whole truth,
For Islam's beauty lies in simplicity, and a heart that's youth.
A smile, a greeting, a lending hand, or a listening ear,
These cost nothing, yet speak volumes, and banish every fear.

Some say it's about the Day of Sacrifice, Eid al-Adha's noble call,
A day to honour Prophet Ibrahim's faith and stand tall.
Some say it's about Rajab's blessings, Shaban's mercy too,
Ramadan's fasting and Eid's joy that shines right through.

It's about Ramadan's blessed month, a time of spiritual rebirth,
A season of fasting, dua, and a deeper connection to Allah's earth.
A time to renew our intentions, to seek forgiveness and to mend,
To strengthen our resolve and to become better versions of ourselves until the end.

It's about charity, with hands that give and hearts that care,
We lift each other, beyond compare.

In acts of kindness, we find our way,
To a beauty that's reflected every day.

The call to prayer, a symphony so sweet,
Echoes through the ages, a summons to meet.
The Adhan's majestic voice, a call to stand as one,
A reminder of our purpose, beneath the radiant sun.

Our beloved Prophet Muhammad (PBUH), a mercy to mankind,
Taught us to live with compassion, and a heart that's aligned.
To care for the orphan, the widow, and the poor,
To stand for justice, and to love, forevermore.

Through his teachings, we learn to be humble and kind,
To forgive and to love, to leave behind the blind.
To strive for excellence in all that we do,
To be the best version of ourselves, for Allah's sake, anew.

It's about Al-Qur'an, a book of guidance true,
A source of wisdom, and a heart that's pure and new.
Its words, a balm to the soul, a healing to the heart,
A reminder of Allah's love, and a brand new start.

Its principles, a beacon of light, in the darkest of nights,
A guiding force that shines so bright and ignites
Justice, compassion, and mercy, a triad of virtue so fine,
A blueprint for living, that's simply sublime.

It's about modesty, a virtue so rare,
A beauty that shines from within, beyond compare.
A strength that's quiet, yet unshakeable and strong,
A heart that's pure, and a spirit that's free and long.

It's about the strength of women, a power so divine,
A source of inspiration, a heart that's truly mine.
From Khadijah's (RA) courage, to Aisha's (RA) wisdom so bright,
To the countless women who shine with faith and light.

It's about men's protection, a safeguard so true,
A responsibility to care and see loved ones through.
To provide, to shield, and to guide with gentle might,
To be a source of comfort and a beacon in the night.

It's about all believing men and women, a bond so strong,
United in faith, with hearts that belong.
Their struggles, their triumphs, their stories untold,
A testament to faith that never grows old.

It's about the gift of children, a blessing so pure,
A trust from Allah (SWT), to nurture, and to ensure.
Their laughter, their smiles, their tiny hands and feet,
A reminder of Allah's love and the beauty that we meet.

It's about families, a bond so strong,
A haven of love, where hearts belong.

A place to grow, to learn, to share and to care,
A reflection of Allah's love and the beauty that's there.

It's about the Ummah, a global family so grand,
United in faith, with a bond that expands.
From east to west, from north to south,
A community of believers, with a shared truth.

Yes, these are part of Islam's beauty, a sacred, blessed design,
But only a part, for Islam's beauty is a tapestry divine.
In words of kindness, love, and peace, we find its gentle hue,
In small gestures of gratitude, and a heart that's pure and true.

In life's precious gifts, like sunrise's glow, and sunset's breeze,
In raindrops' gentle touch, and thunder's mighty seas.
In nature's call, and the wind's soft sigh,
We find Islam's beauty passing us by.

In friendships that stand the test of time,
In families intertwined, a bond that's truly sublime.
In life's ups and downs, we find strength and might,
An appreciation that never ends, a guiding light.

So what is Islam, I ask you, dear friend?
Is it not finding inner strength and living life to the end?
Is it not earning Akhirah's gains, and a heart that's pure and bright?

Is it not placing our Rabb, Al-Wahid, the One True Rabb, in our heart's delight?

The One who guides, protects, and provides, with infinite love and care,
The One who unites us all, as one Ummah, with no divide to share.
So we may be made whole again and find our peaceful nest,
Until we meet at Jannah's gate, where love and joy are at their best.

Can't you see, dear friends, what Islam's beauty truly is?
A way of life, a guiding light, that shines from within and never dims.
A path that's straight, a journey that's true,
A faith that's strong, and a heart that's pure and new.

So let us walk this path, with hearts that are sincere,
With minds that are open and souls that are clear.
Let us strive to be better, to be the best we can be,
To live with kindness, compassion, and humility.

For Islam's beauty is not just a word or a phrase,
It's a way of life, a choice we make every single day.
It's a commitment to love, to care, and to share,
To be a source of comfort and a beacon of hope, beyond compare.

It's a journey of self-discovery, of growth and might,
A path that's guided by the Quran's light.
It's a way of living that's just and fair,
A faith that's rooted in love, and a heart that's full of care.

So let us hold on to this faith, with all our might,
And strive to be the best versions of ourselves, in sight.
Let us spread love, kindness, and compassion wherever we go,
And be a source of peace, in a world that's often slow.

For Islam's beauty is a gift, a treasure so rare,
A way of life that's full of love, and a heart that's full of care.
So let us cherish this gift and hold it dear,
And strive to live our lives, according to Allah's will, year after year.
Ameen.

"And We have certainly honoured the children of Adam" (Quran 17:70)

A divine whisper of self-love, reminding us that we're crafted with care, blessed with potential, and crowned with dignity.

My Message to You

Like stars twinkling in the night sky, our lives are filled with moments of wonder, beauty, and purpose. May the beauty of Islam be the constellation that guides us, and may our hearts be filled with the light of faith, wisdom, and compassion. May this final poem be a reflection of the beauty and honour that lies within us, and may its words inspire us to live with dignity, kindness, and love. May you shine bright like a star, and may your life be a beacon of hope and inspiration to those around you. Ameen.

As We Conclude Part 7

As the final petals of **Part 7** unfold like a rose in full bloom, may the sweet fragrance of **remembrance and gratitude** linger, infusing your heart with the gentle dew of faith, hope, and love. May the Prophetic words, **"Reflect on the blessings of Allah, and do not reflect on the blessings of others"** (Hadith, Narrated by Ibn Majah), be the soft melody that harmonises your soul, guiding you towards a symphony of gratitude and appreciation.

As we conclude this enchanting journey of poetry and reflection, may the wisdom of the Quran's teachings resonate deeply in your heart, nurturing your spirit with the harmony of divine love. May the hidden treasures of faith, resilience, and hope be revealed to you, guiding you through life's triumphs and challenges with courage, wisdom, and compassion.

May our hearts be infused with the nectar of gratitude, and may our words and actions be a shining star of hope and guidance for others. May we trust in Allah's promise, **"And indeed, with hardship comes ease"** (Quran 94:5), and may our faith be the anchor that holds us steadfast in the midst of life's storms.

As we bid farewell to this book, may its lessons and inspiration remain with you, like a gentle breeze that whispers sweet nothings to your soul. May you walk in the light of faith, guided by the wisdom of the Prophetic words, **"The strongest of people are those who are strongest in faith"** (Hadith, Narrated by Al-Bukhari). May your heart be forever changed, like a masterpiece of divine art, and may your life be a testament to the transformative power of faith, hope, and love.

Ameen.

Parting Words

As the final page turns and the curtain falls on this book of poems, I invite you to carry the whispers of faith, love, and resilience with you on your own enchanted journey. May the words within these pages have awakened your heart, nourished your soul, and reminded you of the transformative power of Allah's guidance. May you walk in the gentle light of faith, guided by the wisdom of the Quran and the love of Allah (SWT). May your heart remain filled with gratitude, faith, and devotion to Him, and may you be a source of light, love, and inspiration to those around you, like a beacon of hope in the darkness.

As we bid farewell to this book, I make dua that its lessons and inspiration remain with you, like a gentle breeze that whispers sweet nothings to your soul. May you strive towards personal growth, self-improvement, and spiritual enlightenment, and may your journey be filled with wonder, joy, and love.

May this book of poems be a timeless treasure, leaving a trail of inspiration and guidance for generations to come. May its words be a gentle rain that nourishes the soul, and may its message be a beacon of hope that shines brightly in the darkness. May it be a legacy of love, touching the hearts of all who read it, and may its wisdom and inspiration be a source of comfort, guidance, and solace.

Ya Rabb, I stand before You with a heart overflowing with gratitude and love. Alhamdulillah, from the depths of my soul, for guiding me on this journey, for believing in me, and for showering me with Your unconditional love. Shukran, for the readers who have joined me on this adventure, for the family and friends who have supported me, and for all those who have contributed to making this book a reality.

May Your peace and blessings be upon our beloved Prophet Muhammad (peace be upon him), his family, and all the righteous servants who have walked this path before me. May You bless and reward all those who have been a part of this journey, and may we all be reunited in the hereafter, in the presence of Your divine love.

Ameen., Your Humble Servant, Always and Forever.

www.ingramcontent.com/pod-product-compliance
Lightning Source LLC
Chambersburg PA
CBHW021144160426
43194CB00007B/684